20 BICYCLE TOURS IN VERMONT

The Montgomery, or Lower, covered bridge in Waterville

20 Bicycle Tours in Vermont

JOHN S. FREIDIN   Photographs by the Author

New Hampshire Publishing Company   Somersworth

For my parents   **Doris and Jesse Freidin**
that we might have ridden these roads together

An Invitation to the Reader—Although it is unlikely that the roads you cycle on these tours will change much with time, some road signs, landmarks, and other items may. If you find that changes have occurred on these routes, please let us know so we may correct them in future editions. The author and publisher also welcome other comments and suggestions. Address all correspondence:

Editor, *Bicycle Tours*
New Hampshire Publishing Company
Box 70
Somersworth, NH 03878

International Standard Book Number: 0-89725-000-1
Library of Congress Catalog Card Number: 78-71715
© 1979 by John S. Freidin
Published by New Hampshire Publishing Company
Somersworth, New Hampshire 03878
Printed in the United States of America
Photographs by the author
Back cover photograph by Erik Borg
Design by David Ford

Acknowledgments

The tours are the joint products of all the men and women who have led trips, fixed bicycles, and written letters for Vermont Bicycle Touring; I shall always be in their debt. But special thanks go to Marge Dethloff, Sally Dorsey, and Bruz Brown. For the sake of this book they relieved me of many responsibilities; for the sake of our friendships they ignored my short temper and preoccupation. And without the enthusiastic support of the people who have ridden with Vermont Bicycle Touring, I would have lacked both the incentive and leisure to write. This is their book too.

My research was made immeasurably easier by the previous work of others, but errors of fact and judgment remain fully mine. I relied especially heavily on three books: Ray Bearse, ed., *Vermont: A Guide to the Green Mountain State* (3rd edition, 1968), grandchild of the Federal Writers' Project guide sponsored by the Works Progress Administration of the New Deal; William Hancock *et. al.*, eds., *The Vermont Atlas and Gazetteer* (1978); and Madeleine Kunin and Marilyn Stout, *The Big Green Book: A Four-Season Guide to Vermont* (1976). Finally, for her patience as well as her insight I am grateful to editor Catherine Baker.

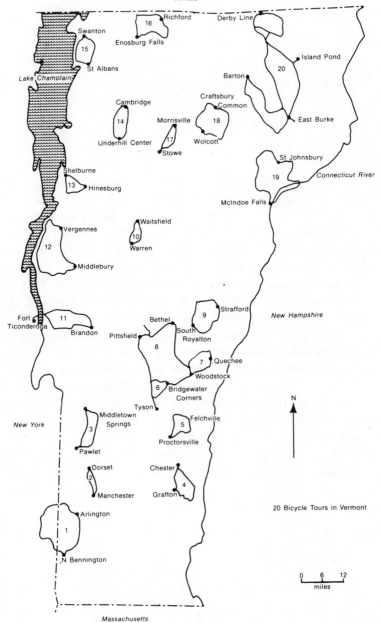

Canada

Richford

Derby Line

16

Swanton

Enosburg Falls

15

Island Pond

St Albans

Barton

20

Lake Champlain

Craftsbury
Common

Cambridge

14

Morrisville

18

East Burke

Underhill Center

17

Wolcott

Stowe

St Johnsbury

Shelburne

19

Connecticut River

13

Hinesburg

McIndoe Falls

Vergennes

Waitsfield

12

10

Warren

Middlebury

New Hampshire

Strafford

9

Bethel

Fort
Ticonderoga

11

South
Royalton

Brandon

Pittsfield

8

Quechee

7

Woodstock

6

Bridgewater
Corners

Tyson

Middletown
Springs

N

New York

3

Felchville

5

Pawlet

Proctorsville

Dorset

Chester

2

4

Manchester

Grafton

20 Bicycle Tours in Vermont

Arlington

1

N Bennington

0   6   12

miles

Massachusetts

Contents

Foreword

Having heard much about the beauties of Vermont, I decided in 1963 to see it for myself. By bicycle, of course.

My trip started at Bantam Lake, Connecticut. From there, it took me through the Berkshires, across the Mohawk Trail, and into the little town of Wilmington, Vermont. It was now late afternoon, and the sky was threatening. If I had had any sense, I would have stayed. But I had read of an interesting old inn in Newfane, and I wanted to sample it.

The ride was much longer than I had imagined it. Hills slowed me down. Halfway, it started to rain, at first a few drops, then a steady downpour, and finally, a veritable deluge. All light was blotted out. On the pitch-black half-flooded road, I was slowed to a crawl. Drenched, blinded, and frozen, I stumbled into Newfane at eight o'clock. Hallelujah. The inn had room for me.

That evening, revived with an excellent dinner, I reflected on the experience. The ride had been a challenge. Even today, I can remember every detail. But I had unnecessarily exposed myself to discomfort, anxiety, even danger. If there had been a John Freidin, I would have planned better.

Bicyclists now have this book to guide them. The tours are described in loving detail, and the countryside is revealed in all its charm. Wish I could follow the trails myself.

Clifford L. Graves, M.D.
Director, International Bicycle Touring Society
La Jolla, California

Introduction

Caterpillars and butterflies. On a ride one day, it struck me that bicyclists could be either one. The difference is their views of the terrain. To caterpillars every hill looks like a mountain, while to butterflies even mountains look level as they float over them. But given time every caterpillar grows into a butterfly. To me this is the greatest beauty of bicycling: that everyone in good health can become a proficient rider simply by doing it. Thanks to the efficiency of bicycles, most cycling requires only a little strength and no agility or speed.

This book is for both caterpillars and butterflies. Whether you have not ridden in years or cycle a thousand miles a season, *20 Bicycle Tours in Vermont* will guide you to routes matching your ability in one of the most exquisite cycling environments imaginable. It will enable you to find your way with confidence; it will alert you to hills and hazards; it will suggest places to swim, find food, and get your bicycle repaired; and it will deepen, I hope, your enjoyment of what you see by telling you a little about the history, architecture, geology, wildlife, and other curiosities along the way.

I have selected the following twenty tours for their beauty and diversity. Each one had to be beautiful; and, as a group, they had to provide a breadth of choices wide enough to suit every level of cyclist and unveil as many facets of Vermont life as possible. In length they range from 16 to 155 miles; in terrain from flat to very hilly. Some tours can be fully enjoyed on a three- or five-speed bicycle; most are best ridden on a ten-speed. The tours are dispersed throughout the state from North Bennington to Derby Line, from

Lake Champlain to the Connecticut River. But every tour ends where it begins. There are overnight tours and day trips, trips to country inns and trips to campgrounds, trips laden with history and trips through remote wonderlands, trips that visit handsome villages and trips that take you swimming, fishing, and bird-watching.

The eight hundred miles covered by these tours all stem from trips run by Vermont Bicycle Touring. By leading those trips since 1972, I have ridden the roads and learned how hundreds of other cyclists, from novices to experts, have felt about them. Their reactions have guided my appraisals of the terrain; their misadventures have helped me compose directions that at last, I hope, are clear to all.

Many places are beautiful, but beauty alone does not satisfy the needs of bicyclists. Vermont is a cyclist's delight not merely because of its beauty, but because of its scale and temperament. Here, where we live in villages not cities, worship in churches not cathedrals, and travel on roads not highways, the environment is scaled to human proportions. Seldom do more than ten miles separate general stores; rarely does a climb remain arduous for more than two miles. The pace of Vermont life more closely resembles the speed of a bicycle than that of an automobile; and the friendliness of the people is more like the cooperation of tandeming than the competitiveness of motoring. To bicycle is to steep yourself in an environment; to do so in Vermont is to fall in love with both the place and the pedaling.

Selecting a Tour

From the state map on page 6, see which tours fall in an area you find interesting or convenient. The tours are grouped into four regions, roughly equal in size, to facilitate your locating them on the map and in the text. Next, look up the tours you are considering to see which suit you in terms of distance and terrain. Then read their introductions, which describe their principal features, and make your choice.

The twenty tours really present far more than twenty choices. A tour is not the same ridden in one season as it is ridden in another; ridden with friends as ridden alone; ridden in the rain as ridden in the sun; ridden when leaves are on trees as ridden when trees are bare. And once you know a ride well in one direction, do it in the other and you will discover a new tour.

For each tour the round-trip distance and the difficulty of the terrain are stated at the beginning of the tour description. The terrain is rated according to the length, steepness, and frequency of the hills you must climb. If you want to know more precisely the nature of the terrain, read the entire tour. There I have tried to describe every hill that is either very steep or lasts at least a mile. But remember, since every tour completes a circle, every inch of climbing is matched by an inch of descent. Furthermore, no two bicyclists make the same assessment of every hill or even find the same hill equally difficult every time they ride it. Here are what my ratings mean:

Easy terrain is generally level and never produces more than one and a half miles of uphill riding for every twenty-five miles of touring. Easy terrain is well suited to three- and five-speed bicycling.

Easy-to-moderate terrain is also generally level but requires one and a half to three miles of climbing for every twenty-five ridden and brings some fast downhill runs. This terrain also suits three- and five-speed bicycling.

Moderate terrain necessitates three to six miles of ascent for each twenty-five miles of riding and is best ridden on a ten-speed bicycle with a low gear in the mid-forties or less.*

Moderate-to-difficult terrain requires climbing three to six miles for roughly every fifteen miles of touring, and the grades are likely to be steeper than on moderate terrain. Gearing reaching into the thirties is helpful.

Difficult terrain also requires three to six miles of climbing for

*To determine the lowest gear on your bicycle count the teeth on the smaller front chain ring, divide that number by the number of teeth on the largest cog of the freewheel, and then multiply the quotient by the diameter, in inches, of the rear wheel.

each fifteen miles of riding, but the hills are often steep. Gearing in the low or mid-thirties is desirable.

I have seen hundreds of people, many with no recent bicycling experience or special conditioning, comfortably ride less than thirty miles over easy or easy-to-moderate terrain. Although the effort tired many of them, fewer than 5 percent had serious difficulty. In age they ranged from seven to seventy.

Preparing for a Tour

Numerous materials have been written on conditioning, equipment, eating, camping, and packing for long bicycle tours. I deal

Across the Missisquoi River to Jay Peak

with these topics only in a very limited way. If you want thorough guidance, write to Bikecentennial or one of the other sources in the Appendix.

The best way to get in shape for bicycling is to bicycle. Other sports, such as tennis or even running, may help, but they do not place identical demands on your body and should not be used as an index of your readiness. To build your stamina, bicycle frequently and regularly—at least two or three times a week—and gradually increase the distance you ride.

Several days before starting a tour carefully read the entire tour description. Decide what to carry with you—such as food and bathing suit—and what to get along the way. The tours are described in a regular pattern. Beside each of the cumulative mileages are the directions you must follow to stay on the route. The mileages are given to help you gauge the times between turns, not to suggest that you use an odometer, though one can be helpful. Most touring cyclists average seven to twelve miles an hour. Advice about terrain, road surface, or places to buy food is stated in one of the paragraphs following the directions that take you there. Similarly, historical, architectural, and other curious information about an area follows the directions that take you there.

Make sure your bicycle is in good repair. Bicycles need overhauling at least every two thousand miles or two years. For safety and ease of operation attention should be paid to brakes, drive train, shifting apparatus, wheels, headset, tires, and the tightness of the seatpost, saddle, and handlebars. Vermont has many bicycle shops, but they are often far from the places you ride on these tours. A list of the closest shops is given at the end of each tour. Before going to a shop, call ahead to make certain it has the parts and expertise you need. Whenever you tour, carry at least a pump and equipment for repairing flat tires.

Saddle soreness is common to cyclists. Within limits you grow accustomed to your perch, and proper pants also help. But the saddle itself makes a major difference, especially for women, since nearly all saddles are designed to fit men. Most touring cyclists, myself included, prefer a leather saddle that has been broken in well or one of the new orthopedically designed models such as those made by Avocet. Avocet has developed a woman's saddle that has been highly praised by virtually every woman I know who has used it.

"A Vermont year is nine months winter and three months damn poor sleddin'." At least according to folklore. Although there are wonderful days for cycling in April and November, the principal bicycling season here runs from early May through the end of October. I like May and June best, because the days are long and the landscape is brilliantly green and strewn with wildflowers. July and August are rarely too hot or humid to be uncomfortable and offer great swimming. The fall foliage season, covering roughly four weeks from mid-September to mid-October, turns the trees into a riot of color, but the likelihood of cold or wet days is greater. Vermont weather is extremely volatile. From May through August daytime temperatures can range from 40° to 90° F. (4° to 33° C.). During September and October they can go from 30° to 80° F. (-1° to 27° C.). Consequently you should prepare yourself for a variety of temperatures even within a single day by dressing in layers.

Select clothing that breathes as well as insulates. Your muscles should be kept warm, especially your legs and knees, and your skin should be kept dry except on the hottest days to prevent the wind from chilling you. Wool is best because it accommodates the widest range of temperatures, dries quickly, and warms you even when it gets wet—although some new synthetic fabrics are supposed to have similar properties.

On bright days carry clothing and lotion to protect yourself from sunburn. A hat with a long bill keeps the sun off your face and the rain off your glasses. To prevent irritation, your pants should have neither seams nor folds that you must sit on. Gloves, especially ones with padded palms, help prevent your hands from numbing and offer some protection if you fall. Better protection comes from cautious cycling and a helmet. Your shoes should tie on snugly— with double knots to prevent a lace from catching in the chain—and have soles adequate to prevent the pedals from hurting your feet. Raingear poses a problem, because most materials that keep the rain out lock the sweat in. In light rains I am most comfortable in one or two wool jerseys. For cold or heavy rain a well-ventilated jacket made of a breathable fabric like Gore-Tex is best. And all your outer clothing ought to be brightly colored—preferably yellow, orange, or red—to make you highly visible.

You should carry water, preferably in a bottle mounted on your bicycle, and a little food. Drink before you are thirsty and eat before you are hungry to keep your strength and spirits up. Good food for snacks include bananas, oranges, granola, nuts, and raisins. You need little protein but lots of fluid plus salts, unrefined sugars, and other carbohydrates. Consider carrying a camera and film; books about birds, wildflowers, or trees; a first-aid kit; a bathing suit; a towel; a pocket knife; and money. Each tour description is accompanied by a sketch map, but an official Vermont state road map would also be helpful (see Appendix).

For day trips you can readily pack what you need in a handlebar bag and in either a rear carrier or a bag that hangs from your saddle. For overnight tours add panniers, which attach to the rear carrier and hang on either side of the rear wheel. In selecting panniers and a rear carrier, insist on equipment that mounts firmly so it cannot under any condition swing into the spokes of your rear wheel.

Doing a Tour

Read the full tour before you start. Then, when you are riding, pause at each turn to read the directions for the next turn, for it may come within a tenth of a mile. All the roads on all the tours are paved unless the directions state that they are not. If you find yourself on an unpaved road not mentioned in the directions, you have gone off course. The text also describes the prominent grades. If nothing is stated about terrain, the road is level or nearly so.

Even more than hills, wind can affect cyclists, for the wind can be your escort, friendly or antagonistic, all day long. Become aware of the wind by watching tall grass and leaves. By recognizing a headwind you can avoid blaming yourself for difficulty that is not your fault. And by recognizing a tailwind you can avoid inflating your ability to the point where you attempt more than you can enjoy.

In order to use the proper muscles, your legs must extend almost fully when the ball of your foot is on the center of the pedal—as it should be when you are cycling—and the pedal is at its lowest point, six o'clock. In that position your leg should bend only slightly at the knee. If it bends more than that, you will tire quickly and be more susceptible to cramps. An easy way to determine the correct height for your saddle is to sit on it, place your heel on a pedal, and then push the pedal to six o'clock. You then should be able to extend your leg fully without having to lock your knee. Make sure whenever you adjust your saddle that you leave at least two inches of seat-post inside the frame.

A ten-speed bicycle is not made to be pedaled as a three-speed. The larger number of gears is designed to conserve your energy by enabling you to keep your legs turning at a relatively constant speed regardless of terrain, wind, or road surface. Once you get the knack, you will find it far less tiring to maintain an even cadence than to change your rate of pedaling, as you must on a three-speed. Furthermore, it is easier to spin your legs quickly, pushing proportionately less strenuously each time, than to turn them slowly and push harder. Yet, nine out of ten inexperienced bicyclists ride in a gear that is at least one step too high. By turning their feet too slowly, they must push harder, and they consequently increase the risk of damaging their knees or straining their leg muscles. If you are a beginner, try to maintain a cadence of forty to sixty revolutions of each foot a minute. As you master that rate, gradually increase your cadence to about eighty, which is excellent for touring. (Bicycle racers spin ninety to one hundred twenty revolutions a minute.)

Cycling on unpaved roads requires special attention and care. Though bicyclists using tubular tires* will have no difficulty

---

*Tubular tires, also called sew-ups, are used mostly by bicycle racers, who prefer them because they are lighter and take more air pressure—hence producing less rolling resistance—than conventional, wired-on tires, often called clinchers. Circular in cross section, tubulars fully enclose their tubes by being sewn together on the inside face. They fasten to the rims of bicycle wheels with glue or two-faced

handling these roads, such riding will inevitably expose their fragile equipment to many sharp pebbles and rocks. To minimize the chance of punctures, all cyclists should keep their tires inflated to the full pressure indicated on the tire and should wipe them free of debris after they are exposed to any material that might cling to them. It is best to use tires that accommodate at least eighty-five pounds of pressure, because they are more resistant to puncture than low-pressure tires and create less rolling resistance.

Vermont law stipulates that "every person riding a bicycle is granted all of the rights and is subject to all of the duties applicable to operators of vehicles, except . . . those provisions which by their very nature can have no application." It also says that cyclists "shall ride as near to the right side of the roadway as practicable," to which I would add a warning not to ride so close to the edge of the pavement that you risk going off it by looking at something other than the road. Vermont law states further that "no person may operate a bicycle unless it is equipped with a bell or other device capable of giving a signal audible for a distance of at least one hundred feet." I do not know whether the human voice qualifies as an "other device"! Several regulations govern bicycling after dark, which it is best not to do at all. Violations of Vermont bicycle laws are punishable by fines of not more than $25 for each offense.

To these laws I would add six which I firmly believe do far more to protect you from accidents: (1) Use a bicycle flag, for it makes you visible to motorists in time for them to deal with your presence on the road; (2) If you wear corrective lenses to drive a motor vehicle, wear them when you bicycle, for you must see at least as well; (3) Ride single file, keeping several bicycle-lengths between you and the cyclist in front of you—and more going downhill—so you do not risk running into one another; (4) Never turn to look behind you while you are operating a bicycle unless you have proven in an open parking lot that you can turn around without permitting your bicycle to alter its course; (5) Never bicycle across railroad

---

sticky tape. Made of extremely light materials, tubulars are more delicate than wired-ons. The relative advantages of tubulars have been greatly reduced by the recent development of lightweight, high-pressure clinchers.

tracks, for in Vermont at least they are considerably higher than the road and very likely to catch your wheel and spill you off the bicycle; (6) MOST IMPORTANT—NEVER make a left turn while you are riding. Stop, get off your bicycle, look, and then walk across, please.

Very few cyclists can conquer every hill. But before walking, try a trick I learned from two Maryland grandmothers. When you reach your lowest gear and can no longer turn the pedals, stop and stand by your bicycle for one minute but no longer. Such pauses, known as "granny stops" by cyclists who have ridden with Vermont Bicycle Touring, relieve your pain and allow your body to gather enough energy to resume pedalling. You can climb nearly any hill more quickly and easily by taking "granny stops" than by pushing your bicycle.

Some dogs like to chase bicycles. Fortunately in Vermont most dogs are tied up and will reach the end of their tethers long before they reach you. However, if a dog does give chase, remember never to change your course to escape, for the dangers of going off the road or into the traffic greatly exceed those posed by the dog. If the dog is very menacing, get off your bicycle, keeping it as a shield between yourself and the animal, and walk out of its turf. Dogs are territorially minded and will not follow you far.

Finally, it is to your advantage not to stop to rest until you have ridden long enough to warm up. That usually takes forty-five minutes to an hour and a quarter. When you do stop, limit your rest to fifteen minutes, for a longer pause cools you so much that you have to begin warming up all over again. This suggestion is emphatically not intended to discourage your stopping to investigate things that interest you or to talk with people along the way. After all, the pleasure of exploring your environment is what bicycle touring is all about.

Southern Vermont

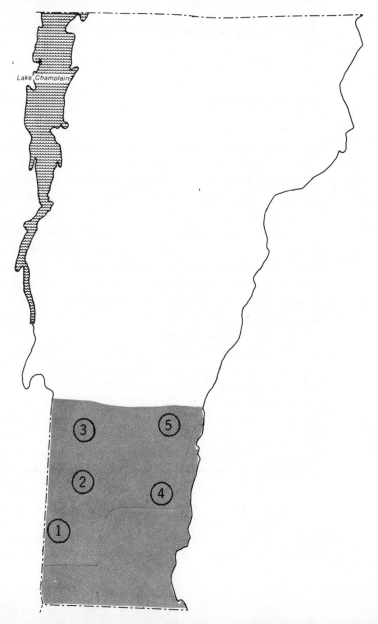

Lake Champlain

Arlington-North Bennington

Moderate terrain; 47 miles

This tour explores Norman Rockwell country in southwestern Vermont and adjacent New York. Taking advantage of three stretches of unpaved road totaling seven and three-quarters miles, the route neatly avoids the region's busy highways. Virtually traffic-free, these unpaved byways connect you more intimately with the natural surroundings than do most paved roads. Following wooded lanes and lush valleys between ridges of the Green and Taconic mountains, the route offers several fine views. If you have the time and a fishing license, you can try your luck in some of the greatest trout water in the country, because for ten miles you cycle along the famous Batten Kill. Or you can swim in that river beneath a red covered bridge by the house where Norman Rockwell lived. The tour also takes you past a reconstructed eighteenth-century country tavern and a hundred-year-old Victorian mansion, both open to the public. You start in Arlington.

0.0 From the Arlington Inn follow US 7 South two hundred yards to the Hawley Furniture showroom (on the right). There turn LEFT onto East Arlington Road toward East Arlington. (No street sign is posted at this corner, but there is a sign for East Arlington.)

Connecticut Anglicans settled Arlington in 1763 so they might enjoy the amenities permitted by their faith in a more tolerant climate than that of puritanical Connecticut. Under their influence Arlington became the first town in Vermont to take such liberties as raising maypoles and decorating Christmas trees.

The St. James Cemetery, behind the stone walls opposite the Arlington Inn, bears witness to the early presence of these Episcopalians. One of Vermont's oldest burial grounds, it contains many curious headstones. Called Tory Hollow during Revolutionary times, Arlington was a Loyalist stronghold but also briefly the residence of Ethan Allen, whose two children and first wife, Mary Brownson, are buried in St. James Cemetery. More recently Arlington has been home to Dorothy Canfield Fisher, the popular chronicler of Vermont life, and Norman Rockwell, whose *Saturday Evening Post* covers depict many local characters.

Since there are no other places to buy food until you reach South Shaftsbury, twelve miles away, you may want to stop at either the Arlington Country Store, beside Hawley Furniture, or Cullinan's Store, which faces East Arlington Road one hundred fifty yards from US 7.

0.8   Turn RIGHT onto Warm Brook Road.

2.0   Turn LEFT onto Maple Hill Road. (At its southern end in South Shaftsbury, this road is called East Road.)

In two-tenths of a mile Maple Hill Road becomes unpaved for five miles. The first three are well packed and shaded; the balance tends to be soft and have small loose rocks on its surface. After a level quarter-mile, Maple Hill Road goes gently but steadily uphill for a mile and a quarter and then flattens out for a mile and a half.

5.2   At the fork bear LEFT to stay on Maple Hill Road, which is still unpaved.

The next mile is the most demanding, for the road ascends more steeply than before just as its surface gets soft. Consequently you may find it difficult to maintain your momentum while preventing your rear wheel from spinning, especially if you stand up on your pedals.

As the slope of the hill tapers off, you reach the Peter Matteson Tavern Museum (on the left), formerly known as Topping Tavern. Records from 1784 indicate that this building served as

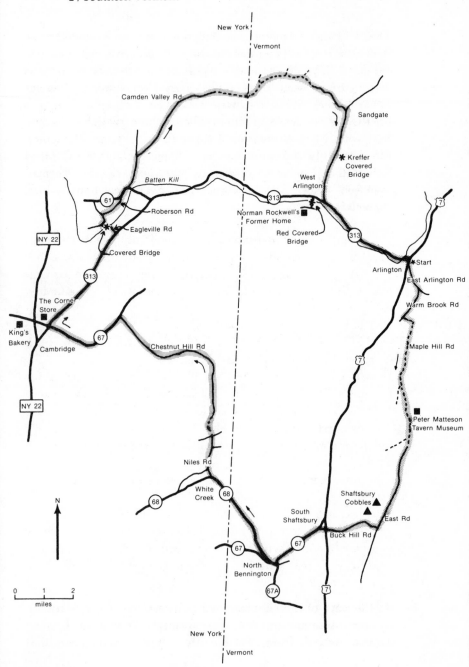

a public house as well as the homestead of a two-hundred-acre farm. Although fire destroyed most of the original structure in 1976, it has since been rebuilt and furnished with early American antiques from the Bennington Museum. The staff, which maintains the museum and works the farm in an eighteenth-century manner, is especially hospitable to people who arrive by bicycle. In fact, given sufficient notice, they will cater a lunch for you. The museum is open between 9:00 a.m. and 5:00 p.m. from April 15 to November 15, except on Mondays and holidays. Admission is $1.50 for adults, $.75 for people aged twelve through seventeen, and free for children.

Beyond the museum, the road climbs gently for slightly under a mile and then becomes paved and level. Two miles after the pavement begins you can see two sharp, knobby hills on your right. Known as the Shaftsbury Cobbles, these limestone hills are worth climbing, if you have the time, for they support several rare ferns and other plants and afford exceptional views of the surrounding countryside.

10.3   At the first paved road on the right, turn RIGHT onto Buck Hill Road. (There is probably no road sign at this corner.)

Buck Hill Road runs rapidly downhill to South Shaftsbury, dropping from a height of 1,200' to 740' in less than two miles.

12.1   At the traffic light in South Shaftsbury, go STRAIGHT across US 7.

12.5   Just after crossing the railroad tracks, bear LEFT onto Route 67 West.

14.5   At the intersection beside the Catamount National Bank (on the right) in North Bennington, turn RIGHT to continue on Route 67 West.

If you follow the signs for the Park-McCullough Mansion from the bank to the corner of West and Park streets, you can visit that elegant Victorian residence. Built in 1865, the thirty-five room mansion exemplifies the extravagant tastes and life style of midnineteenth-century tycoons. It is well worth the time to see its grand stairway, opulent rooms, bizarre furniture, marble mantels, parquet floors, Persian rugs, outdoor sculptures, and collections of carriages and Victorian clothing. Tours of the mansion begin between noon and 4:30 p.m. Sundays through Thursdays from June 10 through October 15. Admission is $1.50 for adults, $1.00 for senior citizens, $.50 for students between six and eighteen, and free for younger children.

14.7 At the fork, bear RIGHT off Route 67 onto the road toward White Creek, New York. (In New York this road is called County Road 68.)

In a mile and a quarter, you cross the state line into New York.

17.0 At the sweeping left curve by the small sign for White Creek, go STRAIGHT off County Road 68 onto Niles Road.

17.3 At the fork, bear RIGHT to continue on Niles Road.

18.2 At the crossroad, go STRAIGHT onto Chestnut Hill Road, which is unpaved for the first three-tenths of a mile.

Just after the road surface becomes paved again, Chestnut Hill Road turns abruptly uphill. The grade is extremely steep but lasts less than three-quarters of a mile.

22.5 At the T, turn LEFT onto Route 67 West.

24.5 At the Stop Sign in Cambridge, New York, turn RIGHT onto Route 313 East.

The Corner Store, directly in front of you at this Stop Sign, treats bicyclists very generously and makes good fresh sandwiches. If you ride past The Corner Store so that the front steps are on your right and continue straight across Route 22 a half-mile into the center of Cambridge, you will find King's Bakery on your left. Their confections are a treat.

29.5 Turn LEFT off Route 313 onto Eagleville Road.

30.0 After going through the covered bridge, turn RIGHT onto the unsigned road.

30.4 At the first paved road on the right, turn RIGHT onto Roberson Road. (No street sign is posted at this turn.)

31.1 Bear RIGHT onto County Road 61. (There is probably no route marker at this turn.)

31.5 At the corner where County Road 61 turns right to cross the Batten Kill, go STRAIGHT onto the unsigned road.

32.2 At the fork, bear RIGHT onto Camden Valley Road and follow the signs for Sandgate and Camden Valley Road for eight miles.

In three and a quarter miles the pavement ends. Camden Valley Road is then unpaved but well packed and smooth for two and a half miles, which slope gently uphill. A quarter-mile after the surface becomes paved again, the road shoots sharply downhill through a series of tight S-curves usually littered with loose gravel. These conditions last three-quarters of a mile and must be ridden cautiously. After the curves, the road continues moderately downhill for one and a quarter miles more.

40.2   At the T in Sandgate, which is merely an intersection, turn RIGHT toward Arlington and Route 313.

For the next three miles you descend gently, almost without

On the side road to Norman Rockwell's old home

pause, back to the Batten Kill. About halfway down you pass the Kreffer covered bridge on your left. In 1977 designer Susan DePeyster and carpenter William Skidmore converted an open-planked bridge spanning the Green River here into this short covered bridge.

43.4   At the Stop Sign in West Arlington, which is also only an intersection, turn LEFT onto Route 313 East.

If you would like to swim by a beautiful red covered bridge, built in 1852, or see the house where Norman Rockwell lived, do not turn left at this Stop Sign. Instead turn right and ride a half-mile west on Route 313. The swimming beneath the eighty-foot bridge over the Batten Kill is excellent and can be reached either by walking into the water from the sandy shore at the far end of the bridge or by swinging from a rope which hangs from the bridge. If you ride through the bridge a quarter-mile to the T, the house facing you on the right is the one Norman Rockwell occupied. It is now privately owned and not open to visitors.

47.0   At the Stop Sign, you are at the junction of Route 313 and US 7, opposite the Arlington Inn, where the tour began.

Bicycle Shops
Giard's Bike Shop, 208 North Street, Bennington, VT   (802-442-3444)
The Bicycle Shop, Routes 11 & 30, Manchester Center, VT   (802-362-1625)
Up and Downhill, Inc., 160 Ben Mont Avenue, Bennington, VT   (802-442-8664)

2

Dorset-Manchester

Easy terrain; 25 miles

For over a century genteel colonial and Victorian residences have
made Dorset and Manchester summer, and more recently winter,
retreats for cosmopolitan Easterners. Following shaded backroads
past magnificent homes and then skirting open fields at the bases
of Mount Equinox (el. 3,816') and Mother Myrick Mountain
(el. 3,290'), this route leads also to many distinctive shops and cultural attractions, such as the Southern Vermont Art Center and
the Dorset Playhouse. Well-groomed farms of horse and cattle
breeders nestle beneath the mountains aligning the valley where
you bicycle along the Batten Kill. And marvelous swimming awaits
you at the old marble quarry in Dorset. The tour begins and ends
by the village green in Dorset.

0.0 Leave Dorset on Church Street, which runs west from Route 30
between the village green and the Dorset Inn.

The Dorset Inn (1796) serves wholesome New England fare and
welcomes bicyclists. If you are looking for food to carry with you,
you can buy a freshly made sandwich and choose from a wide
selection of other foods at Peltier's General Store, directly
across the green from the inn.

Originally a center of trade and finance for local farmers, Dorset
has grown over the last hundred years into a community of
wealthy seasonal residents, retired persons, and other ex-
urbanites. They have meticulously preserved the town's archi-

tecture and brought it a cultural vitality that supports a summer theater, a dance program, and several antique and craft galleries. The United Church of Dorset and East Rupert (1912), on your left as you leave town, is built of Dorset marble and decorated with stained glass windows that depict local pastoral scenes. The Dorset Playhouse can be found on Cheney Road a block south of the church.

1.0   At the Stop Sign, turn LEFT onto West Road.

In a mile and a half at the corner of West and Nichols Hill roads

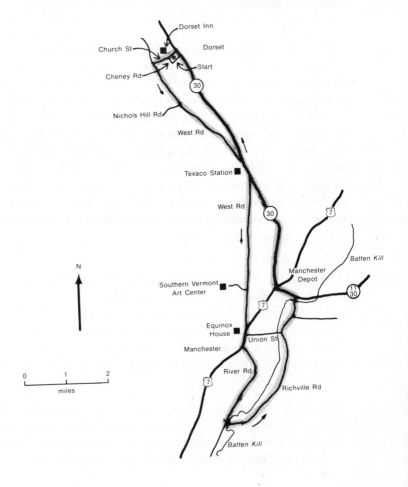

you pass on your right a state historical plaque marking the site of the Cephas Kent Tavern. There in 1776 Ethan Allen's Green Mountain Boys proclaimed Vermont's independence of New Hampshire and New York. From 1777 until 1791, when it became the fourteenth state, Vermont was an independent republic.

5.0 At the Stop Sign, turn RIGHT onto Route 30 South.

5.6 Just beyond the Texaco station (on the right), turn RIGHT onto West Road.

Within a half-mile, you begin climbing the only hill on this tour. It rises gradually with occasional level stretches for a mile and a half. After the plateau at the top, you ride downhill nearly two miles to Manchester. Halfway down this hill on your right is the entrance to the Southern Vermont Art Center, which offers concerts as well as exhibitions of the work of local artists. Its Garden Cafe serves lunch from 11:30 a.m. to 3:00 p.m., and reservations are advised. For reservations and information about concerts and exhibitions, call (802-362-1405). From the first weekend in June until mid-October, the center is open from 10:00 a.m. to 5:00 p.m., Tuesdays through Saturdays, noon to 5:00 p.m. on Sundays, and 10:00 a.m. to 5:00 p.m. on those Mondays that are holidays. Admission is $1.00 for adults, $.50 for students, and free for children under twelve.

9.7 At the Stop Sign in Manchester, go STRAIGHT onto US 7 (Main Street) South.

Immediately on your right, beside the Johnny Appleseed Bookshop, and behind a sidewalk of marble slabs, stands the white, columned Equinox House. This formerly elegant hotel, currently closed and in poor repair, provided its Victorian guests with stables and horse carriage service to and from the railroad station in Manchester Depot.

10.0 Turn LEFT onto River Road.

River Road begins with a fast, curving descent that grows gentle after a half-mile and lasts a total of two miles.

12.5 Beside a white farmhouse (on the right), turn LEFT toward Manchester Depot onto Richville Road, the first possible left turn off River Road. (There may be no street sign at this intersection.)

You immediately cross a bridge over the Batten Kill, one of Vermont's most prolific wild trout streams.

17.0   At the tiny traffic island, bear LEFT to stay on Richville Road.

17.5   At the Stop Sign in Manchester Depot, turn LEFT onto Route 30 North (also Route 11 West).

18.0   At the traffic light, turn RIGHT to stay on Route 30 North, which at this point is also US 7.

Along US 7, within a mile north and south of this intersection you can find most of Manchester's galleries, shops, and eating places. This stretch of highway is not well suited for bicycling, because it is heavily traveled and narrow. Should you wish to browse in the village, you can safely leave your bicycle locked in this area and walk.

Riding Route 30 near Dorset

18.2   At the traffic light, turn LEFT to stay on Route 30 North.

In about four and a half miles, opposite a one-story building called the Dorset Shops, a path on the right side of Route 30 leads to the Dorset quarry, at its opening in 1758 the first commercial marble quarry in America. Dorset marble has been used for public buildings not only in Vermont but throughout the country. However for years no mining has taken place here, and the quarry, now filled with spring water, makes a beautiful swimming hole. Actually there are two quarries—one within fifty yards of the road and a second, popular with skinny-dippers, about a hundred yards beyond the first. Both are open to the public for unsupervised swimming.

25.0   When you reach the Dorset Inn (on the left), you are back where the tour began.

Bicycle Shops

Green Mountain Schwinn Cyclery, 133 Strongs Avenue, Rutland, VT (802-775-0869)

Sports Peddler, 162 North Main Street (US 7), Rutland, VT   (802-775-0182)

The Bicycle Shop, Routes 11 & 30, Manchester Center, VT   (802-362-1625)

3

Pawlet-Middleton Springs

Difficult terrain; 30 miles

Following very quiet roads through pastoral countryside, this tour begins in Pawlet and visits the small Victorian resort of Middletown Springs. The healing powers of the iron and sulphur springs in Middletown drew nineteenth-century ladies and gentlemen to "take the waters" nearly a century ago. Although the springs have not been in commercial use for a long while, the springhouse beside a fern-lined brook was recently rebuilt and makes a delightful resting place. Rolling farmlands stretch from the road's edge to sugarbushes on the foothills of the surrounding Taconic and Green mountains. There are a few long views of these two mountain ranges, but generally the setting is intimate rather than grand.

0.0 Leave the intersection in Pawlet by heading north on Route 133 toward Middletown Springs.

Set at the convergence of Flower Brook and the Mettawee River, Pawlet prospered as a mill town a hundred and fifty years ago. At the falls in the center of this tiny village stands a handsome, though idle, waterwheel, twenty-seven feet in diameter and four feet wide. Johnny Mach built the wheel during the depression of the 1930s to supply his general store and home with electricity.

1.0 At the fork, turn LEFT to stay on Route 133 North.

Within a mile you begin climbing a two-mile hill. From the top the road descends for one and a half miles and then rolls more up than down the rest of the way to Middletown Springs. As you enter the village of Middletown Springs, a small unpaved road leads off the right side of Route 133 to the town park and restored springhouse. The stream is too shallow for swimming but makes a delightful place to cool off and refill your water bottle. You can buy a snack either at the general store on the right just before the turn-off for the springhouse or at Grant's Store opposite the village green.

11.0 At the Stop Sign in Middletown Springs, turn RIGHT to stay on Route 133 North, which at this intersection merges with Route 140 East.

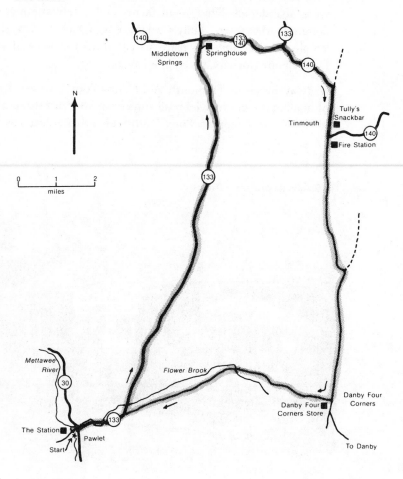

13.0   At the fork, bear RIGHT onto Route 140 East.

Much of the next three miles goes uphill.

16.0   At Tinmouth, just beyond Tully's Snack Bar (on the left), go STRAIGHT off Route 140 onto the unsigned road that leads to Danby Four Corners. As soon as you leave Route 140, you pass on your left the garage of the Tinmouth Volunteer Fire Department. For the next seven miles, follow the signs for Danby and Pawlet.

Tinmouth served as a small iron manufacturing center with its own furnace and forges from the 1780s until 1837, when they were abandoned. Now small farms and a few summer homes dominate the town. Tully's Snack Bar, which serves pleasant, simple food, is the last place to eat until the general store at Danby Four Corners, seven miles away.

Midway between Tinmouth and Danby Four Corners, by a row of mailboxes, an unpaved road runs from your left three-quarters of a mile to Chipman Pond. Although private cottages occupy

The Station Restaurant in Pawlet

most of the shoreline, there are spots where the lake is accessible to the public, should you wish to go swimming.

23.0   At the intersection in front of Danby Four Corners Store, turn RIGHT onto another unsigned road so that you pass the front of the store on your left. Look carefully for this turn to avoid riding to Danby, which lies four miles downhill off the route.

Just beyond Danby Four Corners you begin the final climb of the tour. You must pedal uphill for about one and a half miles, but then you begin a long beautiful descent that extends nearly without interruption all the way back to Pawlet.

29.0   At the Stop Sign, go STRAIGHT onto Route 133 South toward Pawlet.

30.0   At the Stop Sign, you're back in Pawlet where you began.

Flower Brook offers excellent swimming just upstream of Johnny Mach's old waterwheel below the bridge in Pawlet. It is easiest to reach the water from the north side of the river by the post office. Seventy-five yards along a side road west of Route 30 The Station Restaurant, built in an old train station and decorated with railroading memorabilia, serves delicious ice cream and sandwiches.

Bicycle Shops

Green Mountain Schwinn Cyclery, 133 Strongs Avenue, Rutland, VT (802-775-0869)

Sports Peddler, 162 North Main Street (US 7), Rutland, VT   (802-775-0182)

The Bicycle Shop, Routes 11 & 30, Manchester Center, VT   (802-362-1625)

Chester-Grafton

Easy-to-moderate terrain; 26 miles

Starting by the long, slender green that splits the main street of Chester, this tour passes some of Vermont's most beautiful early architecture and affords a chance of seeing a steam train in operation. Following the broad shoulder of the Calvin Coolidge Memorial Highway southeast through the Williams River valley, the route comes to an interesting eighteenth-century burial ground and provides delightful views of rocky pastures and rolling hills. It then turns south onto a small road through woods of sugar maples only occasionally interrupted by the clearing of a small farm. Changing direction again outside the village of Saxtons River, the tour continues west on a narrow and winding old stagecoach road that draws you into the scenes it passes as if no road existed at all. Then, after a pause in the jewellike town of Grafton, you head back to the stone house village of Chester, where you may complete the day with a fine dinner at the Chester Inn.

0.0   From the Chester green follow Route 11 (Main Street) East.

In the early part of the nineteenth century a family of masons by the name of Clark settled in Chester and turned its talents to building stone houses. Constructed of locally quarried gray-green granite, these gracious but unpretentious homes make Chester a special place. Often a full two and a half stories high, many contain secret rooms where before the Civil War blacks seeking freedom from slavery hid as they fled northward on the underground railway. Most of the stone houses face Route 103, both north and south of its intersection with Route 11.

If you like maps, do not miss the National Survey Company, headquartered in Chester. The Survey's excellent maps are sold and displayed in its office on Main Street. Chester has a good bakery and several groceries, although you need not carry much food along since you can shop or eat at restaurants in both Saxtons River and Grafton.

0.7   At the intersection, continue STRAIGHT off Route 11 onto Route 103 South, the Calvin Coolidge Memorial Highway.

As you cycle down the wide shoulder of Route 103, you may catch a glimpse of an old railroad train puffing its way along the Williams River. With whistle blowing and bell ringing, the nostalgic steam train, like yourself, is following a route developed by Indians as a footpath and used by the colonists as a bridle path and military road. In 1849 the Rutland Railroad Company laid tracks over that path to link Rutland with Boston, thereby creating a new market for Vermont dairy products. The train you may see comes from the Steamtown Museum, the largest collection of steam locomotives and equipment in the world. Located on the Connecticut River north of Bellows Falls, Steamtown is open daily from 9:00 a.m. to 6:00 p.m. between Memorial Day and October 15. Admission is $5.95 for adults and $3.25 for children under twelve, and covers an hour-and-a-quarter train ride as well as the museum's hundred exhibits, which include a working turntable, over forty locomotives, and many sleepers, cabooses, and private railroad cars. In addition to its regular excursions, Steamtown runs a fall foliage special, a "Steam in the Snow" trip, and a "Railfans' Weekend." For more information, write to the Steamtown Foundation, P.O. Box 71, Bellows Falls, VT 05101.

Four and a half miles from Chester the Rockingham Meeting House perches on a knoll to your right just off Route 103. Built in 1787 this meeting house remains one of the best examples of early church architecture in New England. It is a two-story frame clapboard structure with seven bays, a modillioned cornice, and

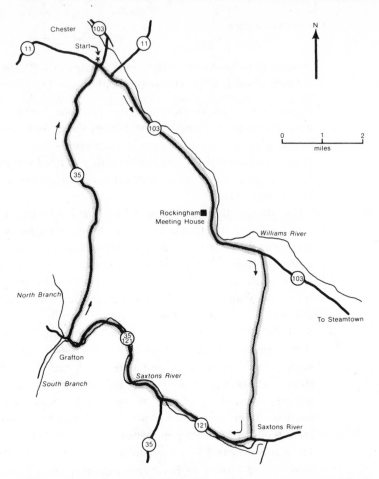

a gable roof. Inside are a high pulpit and box pews. Around back lies the old cemetery, which contains some of the most interesting gravestone carvings in Vermont. The carvings are delicately etched on fragile, weathered slate, so if you make rubbings treat the stones very gently.

7.0   Turn RIGHT toward Saxtons River. (Although this road is unnamed and unnumbered, it is clearly marked by a sign on the right for Saxtons River.)

12.0   At the Stop Sign on the outskirts of Saxtons River, turn sharply RIGHT onto Route 121 West.

Route 121 is narrow and winding. On the curves ride carefully close to the edge of the pavement, because the bends in the road often prevent motorists from seeing you until they are practically on top of you. Here you are following an old stagecoach road along the Saxtons River, a challenging white-water run in early spring.

If you would like a delicious lunch served in a cheery, handsome setting, turn left instead of right at this stop sign and ride a half-mile to the Saxtons River Inn. In 1903 this building was built as an inn but then served as a private home for many years before being imaginatively reconverted to an inn in 1974. It is on the left side of Main Street as you enter town.

Before leaving Saxtons River you might enjoy looking at the old country kitchen and excellent early photographs maintained by the Saxtons River Historical Society and displayed on the ground floor of West Church. The collection is open from July 1 to September 15 on Saturdays, Sundays, and holidays between 2:30 p.m. and 5:00 p.m. There are also two antique shops and a general store on Main Street.

15.0   At the T in Cambridgeport, turn RIGHT to continue toward Grafton on Route 121 West, which here joins Route 35 North.

19.0   At Grafton, turn RIGHT onto Route 35 North toward Chester.

The story of Grafton bears telling, because it is unique. Surrounded by low-lying hills at the confluence of the Saxtons River's two branches, Grafton has ridden the crests of prosperity and the troughs of depression. In the 1820s nearly fifteen hundred people lived there and thrived on the profits of thirteen soapstone quarries and many water-powered mills, including two which loomed the fleece of some ten thousand sheep pastured on the surrounding hillsides. As Grafton flourished, its people built themselves not only churches and private homes of fine design and workmanship, but a magnificent inn, now called the Old Tavern. With this facility Grafton became a town of distinction, hosting over the years such prominent guests as Henry Thoreau, Ulysses Grant, Theodore Roosevelt, Woodrow Wilson, and Rudyard Kipling.

But near the end of the century decline set in. Sheep farmers moved west in search of fresh grazing land, and woolen mills moved south in search of cheap labor. One by one the industries that had produced Grafton's wealth disappeared. By the end of the Great Depression fewer than four hundred persons called Grafton home, and nearly all eighty houses in the village were up for sale at rock bottom prices.

Then, in 1963, thanks to the great foresight and generosity of Pauline Dean Fiske, the Windham Foundation was born. Its purpose is no less than the town's resuscitation; its means the purchase of real estate and the restoration of buildings. Over the past fifteen years the Foundation has bought and rehabilitated more than twenty buildings, including the Old Tavern, the Village Store, a dairy farm, a blacksmith's shop, and several private houses, many of which are now leased to their former owners. To bolster the town's economy, the Foundation created the Grafton Village Cheese Company, and to protect open lands it acquired over a thousand acres around the village. That land is maintained for wildlife conservation, hiking, and cross-country skiing. This massive, continuing effort has brought Grafton out of a long sleep into a new, but very different, life. Though many jobs have been created, the success of the Foundation has pushed the price of real estate beyond the reach of many former residents, and once again turned the Old Tavern into a gracious and friendly inn, but one which few can afford. Newcomers have moved in, and many oldtimers have left.

Still, Grafton is not a museum-town. It is a lively place where people live and work and govern themselves by town meeting. Most of the buildings are not open to the public because they are privately occupied. But much of interest is visible from the outside, and several buildings can be visited. Information and maps are available at the front desk of the Old Tavern. Along the side streets you can find several art galleries and antique shops plus two covered bridges. The Village Store extends a warm welcome to bicyclists and sells fine sandwiches as well as

Approaching Grafton on Route 121

a good selection of fresh fruit, wines, Grafton cheese, and fudge. The store keeps long hours every day but Sunday, when it closes at 1:00 p.m.

Immediately upon leaving Grafton on Route 35 North, you climb a steep but short hill. After a half-mile the slope tapers off to a gentle grade lasting a mile and a half. Then, after passing through woods, the road turns a corner and descends quickly two and a half miles into Chester.

25.7 At the Stop Sign, turn LEFT onto Route 11.

26.0 You are at the Chester green, where you began the tour.

Bicycle Shops

A. B. Carpenter, Route 103 (North Street), Chester Depot, VT   (802-875-2676)

Fleming Schwinn, 1-3 Putney Road, Brattleboro, VT   (802-254-6095)

Ingenuity Shops Ltd., Putney Road, Brattleboro, VT   (802-257-0919)

Red Circle, Inc., 60 Elliot Street, Brattleboro, VT   (802-254-4933)

The Cyclery Plus, US 4, West Woodstock, VT   (802-457-3377)

West Hill Shop, Depot Street, Putney, VT   (802-387-5718)

West Hill Shop, Harmony Place, Brattleboro, VT   (802-257-7080)

5

Proctorsville-Felchville

Moderate terrain; 26 miles

Starting in the old mill town of Proctorsville, this tour carves a circle through hardwood forests and quiet farmlands. No important towns, museums, or historical sites border the route; its attraction lies in the beauty of the countryside around you. Bicycling nearly the entire way within sight of rivers or streams, you twice have good places to swim. The tour's only difficult stretch—three and a half miles uphill along a sometimes rough, unpaved road—comes near the beginning and is amply rewarded by delightful views of a peaceful valley and the charm of a road shaded by a canopy of trees. Otherwise the terrain is easy and includes a six-mile descent. If you are seeking a genuinely pastoral ride, this tour is hard to beat.

0.0 From Gilcris' Store in Proctorsville, follow Route 131 East.

0.3 Turn LEFT off Route 131 onto Twenty Mile Stream Road.

A half-mile outside Proctorsville, Twenty Mile Stream Road ascends steeply for a half-mile and then gradually for three miles more. The next three and a half miles, which are unpaved, climb steadily up a moderate to steep grade. Though the road surface is well packed, loose rocks and washboardlike bumps occasionally slow you down.

Three-quarters of a mile from Proctorsville watch the left side of Twenty Mile Stream Road for a sign resembling a football with two diagonal stripes in the middle. It marks the entrance to the Proctorsville Pottery, where potter Alan Regier keeps shop from 10:00 a.m. to 6:00 p.m., Fridays, Saturdays, and Sundays between

July 4 and Labor Day and during the fall foliage season. You may arrange a visit at other times by calling Regier at 802-226-7331.

7.0   At the T, turn RIGHT onto Kingdom Road, which is the first paved road you reach after Twenty Mile Stream Road becomes unpaved. (No road sign is posted at this turn.)

For three-quarters of a mile, Kingdom Road goes gently uphill. Then it turns sharply downhill and carries you to Felchville (Reading P.O.). If you maintain a slow speed, you can pick your own swimming hole in the North Branch of the Black River.

13.7 At the Stop Sign in Felchville (Reading P.O), turn RIGHT onto Route 106 South.

Before leaving Felchville, if you are the least bit hungry, go into Ryan's Store, on your left when you reach this Stop Sign. Ryan's

Cycling by one of the gingerbread houses in Cavendish

has been catering to the needs of bicyclists for many years and during that time cheered up more than one cold and wet rider. The store makes incredibly generous sandwiches to your specifications and has a good selection of wines, fresh fruit, and other groceries. You can picnic on the lawn of the town hall across the street from Ryan's or by the Black River.

The Reading Historical Society Museum beside the town library on Route 106 contains old furniture, clothing, paintings, photographs, and an unusual collection of advertising cards and old music. Between mid-May and October the museum opens on Wednesday afternoons from 2:00 to 5:00 and by appointment (802-484-7286).

17.8   At the blinker in Downers, turn RIGHT onto Route 131 West.

In three-tenths of a mile, look carefully to your left for a small unpaved road leading diagonally off Route 131. If you follow that

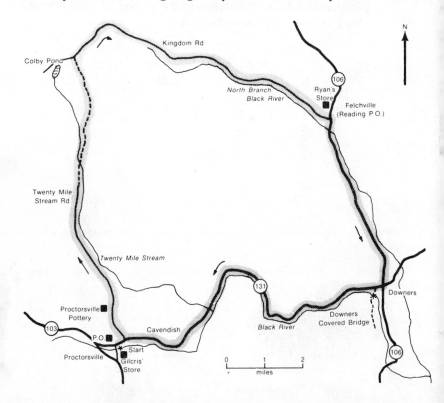

road two hundred yards, you will find the Downers covered bridge, built around 1840. Below it lies a shallow, pleasant swimming hole in the Black River.

Six miles west of Downers, just after you have ridden up a short rise that is the only significant incline on Route 131, you come into the small town of Cavendish. Cavendish has several marvelous gingerbread houses and an old stone meetinghouse as well as two small general stores, all of which face Route 131. Cavendish's most famous resident by far is Alexander Solzhenitsyn.

26.0   You are back in Proctorsville, where this tour began.

Bicycle Shops

Bixby's Bicycle Shop, Route 103, Ludlow, VT   (802-228-3532)

Green Mountain Schwinn Cyclery, 133 Strongs Avenue, Rutland, VT (802-775-0869)

Sports Peddler, 162 North Main Street (US 7), Rutland, VT   (802-775-0182)

The Cyclery Plus, US 4, West Woodstock, VT   (802-457-3377)

Central Vermont

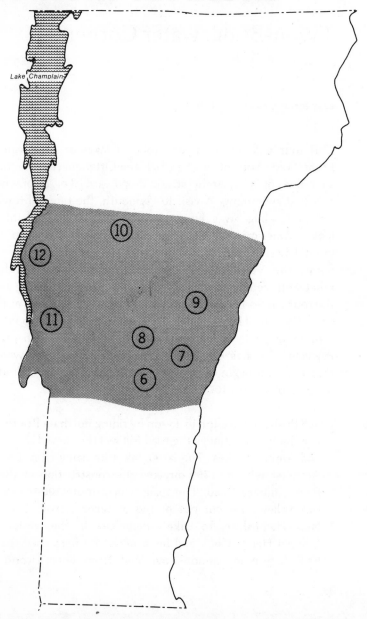

Lake Champlain

6

Tyson-Bridgewater Corners

Easy terrain; 29 or 19 miles

This tour will please anyone fond of lakes or American history. From Tyson you follow the Black and Ottauquechee rivers and the shorelines of Echo, Amherst, and Woodward lakes, all of which offer excellent swimming. A visit to Plymouth, the tiny hill town where Calvin Coolidge was born, provides a nostalgic and informative look at American country life fifty to a hundred years ago. The Vermont Division of Historic Sites carefully maintains the Coolidge home, the Vermont Farmers Museum, and several other early nineteenth-century buildings in Plymouth. By starting in Tyson, the tour passes Echo and Amherst lakes twice and puts at the trail's head the fine facilities of Echo Lake Inn: a dining room, lounge, swimming pool, tennis court, and lakeside dock with canoes and rowboats. Cyclists who prefer a nineteen- rather than twenty-nine-mile tour can begin by the Salt Ash Inn in Plymouth Union at the junction of Routes 100 and 100A (mileage 5.0 below).

0.0   Leave the Echo Lake Inn in Tyson by riding north on Route 100.

      For the first two miles the road follows the curved shores of Echo and Amherst lakes. The latter takes its name from Lord Jeffrey Amherst who in 1759 directed the construction of the Crown Point Military Road. The road, which Route 100 traces through this valley, was cut out of the wilderness from Charlestown, New Hampshire, to Lake Champlain. In the winter of 1775 Colonel Henry Knox and his army of farmers used the road to haul fifty-nine cannons overland from Fort Ticonderoga to

Boston, where they played a critical role in driving out the British. Both Amherst and Echo lakes offer excellent swimming, best reached from the public boat launching ramps along their shores.

5.0   Turn RIGHT onto Route 100A.

Immediately the road curves up what many bicyclists call Hysteria Hill. Although barely a half-mile long, it is heart-pounding steep. However, once you reach the top, Route 100A takes you delightfully downhill for nearly six miles.

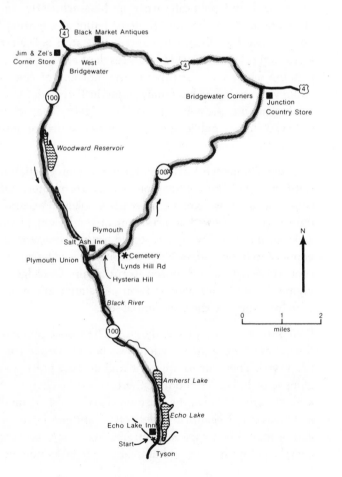

6.0   Four-tenths of a mile beyond the crest of Hysteria Hill and just
past a pond on your right, turn LEFT onto the road to Plymouth
and ride a half-mile to that village.

On Independence Day, 1872, in a weathered cottage attached to
the general store in Plymouth, the thirtieth president of the
United States, Calvin Coolidge, was born. (Only one other Vermonter, Chester A. Arthur, has occupied the presidency.) After
completing secondary school at Black River Academy in nearby
Ludlow, Coolidge attended Amherst College and then embarked
on a legal and political career in Massachusetts. Inaugurated
governor in 1919, he quickly drew national attention by calling
out the National Guard to supress a Boston police strike. Only
a year later, he was elected vice-president as Warren G. Harding's
running mate. Then, at three in the morning of August 3, 1923,
while vacationing at his family home in Plymouth, Coolidge was
awakened with the news of Harding's death. The vice-president's
father, a notary public, immediately swore his son into office as
president.

Coolidge completed Harding's term and won election in his own
right in 1924. The taciturn, penurious Vermonter—whose cam-
paign slogan was "Keep Cool with Coolidge"—seems an ironic
figure to have served as president at the height of the Roaring
Twenties. But he loyally supported big business, and the nation's
booming economy lifted his popularity. Indeed he might well have
been reelected had he chosen to run again. Coolidge is buried at
Plymouth beside his wife and son in a simple grave adorned only
with his name and the presidential seal.

Plymouth deserves a leisurely visit. The Coolidge homestead and
the cottage where the president was born have been meticulously
preserved. Their furnishings and architecture present an accurate
glimpse of life in Vermont at the turn of the century. Nearby, in
a mammoth old barn, the Vermont Farmers Museum displays an
instructive and beautiful collection of antique farm implements.
These tools seem especially interesting today, because they accomplished by human and animal power tasks now done almost

exclusively by electricity and fossil fuels. From late May until mid-October, these buildings are open to the public seven days a week from 9:30 a.m. to 5:30 p.m. Admission is $1; children under fourteen are not charged.

Along the shore of Echo Lake

Across from the Coolidge home stands the Union Christian Church (1840). Its exterior resembles those of many other clapboard churches in Vermont. But its interior was ingeniously rebuilt in 1890 out of rare, local hard pine in a style known as carpenter Gothic, because it achieves with wood the Gothic forms normally constructed from stone. The new Calvin Coolidge Memorial Center displays a notable collection of late nineteenth- and early twentieth-century photographs, mostly related to the life of Calvin Coolidge and captioned with quotations from his autobiography. At the north end of the village, the Plymouth Cheese Corporation merits a visit, especially on weekdays when you can see its unique curd cheese being made. The village also contains a small restaurant, picnic tables, and two shops that sell local crafts.

7.0 Retrace your way from Plymouth to the Stop Sign at Route 100A and turn LEFT onto Route 100A toward Woodstock.

The village cemetery where Coolidge is buried sits a quarter-mile away from this intersection on a pretty knoll overlooking the surrounding hills. To get to the cemetery, rather than turning onto Route 100A go straight across it onto Lynds Hill Road. After your visit retrace your way back to Route 100A and turn right onto it. Route 100A follows Broad Brook gently downhill for nearly six miles.

13.0 At the Stop Sign in Bridgewater Corners, turn LEFT onto US 4 West.

The Junction Country Store, which occupies a corner at this intersection, sells a fine selection of food, drink, and unusual country merchandise. Bicyclists are always welcomed. US 4 is more heavily traveled than other roads on this tour, but it is wide and offers a paved shoulder most of the way. The Black Market, on your right in five and a half miles, sells fine antiques and makes an interesting stopping place.

19.0 At the blinker in West Bridgewater, turn LEFT onto Route 100 South and follow it to your starting point (either five miles to Plymouth Union or ten to Tyson).

On your right immediately after turning onto Route 100 stands

Jim & Zel's Corner Store, which makes good fresh sandwiches. Directly behind the store, The Back Behind Saloon, dimly lit and decorated with antiques, serves good lunches and dinners.

The first two miles of Route 100 go gradually uphill to the northern end of Woodward Reservoir, where swimming is permitted. Within two hundred yards after the lake comes into sight watch for the turn-out for cars and a boat launching ramp. The mowed grass along the lakeshore here makes a delightful spot to relax and picnic.

24.0 The Salt Ash Inn in Plymouth Union at the junction of Routes 100 and 100A is on your left.

29.0 The Echo Lake Inn in Tyson is on your right.

Bicycle Shops

Bixby's Bicycle Shop, Route 103, Ludlow, VT   (802-228-3532)

Green Mountain Schwinn Cyclery, 133 Strongs Avenue, Rutland, VT (802-775-0869)

Sports Peddler, 162 North Main Street (US 7), Rutland, VT   (802-775-0182)

The Cyclery Plus, US 4, West Woodstock, VT   (802-457-3377)

7

Woodstock-Quechee

Moderate terrain; 24.5 miles

This tour combines village elegance and rural tranquility. It starts in Woodstock, where Vermont's most stately architecture has been meticulously preserved. Although the village often bustles with traffic and pedestrians by late morning, the route neatly avoids that commotion by following rarely used roads through the quiet countryside north of town. With the exception of a single difficult hill, three miles long but conveniently located near the beginning of the route, the tour is not demanding and features one of the state's finest downhill runs, nearly seven miles long. Slightly over two miles at the tour's end are not paved, but they suit two-wheel travel well and should pose no problem even to cyclists using tubular tires.

0.0   From the Woodstock green follow Route 12 (Elm Street) North toward Barnard.

Before leaving, take at least a quick tour of town by bicycle or foot. Vermont's most distinguished nineteenth-century townhouses line Woodstock's oval green and shaded side streets. Since 1786 the shire town of Windsor County, Woodstock has always managed to be a center of wealth and gracious living and always avoided being a place for manufacturing. Finance and commerce, not industry, have kept this town both prosperous and beautiful. Perhaps its former wealthy residents shielded Woodstock from change; certainly its most recent residents have done so. Telephone and electrical wires are buried; signs are kept to a minimum; and in 1969, when a new bridge was needed to cross the Ottaquechee River, the town built a covered bridge in authentic Town Lattice style, using only wooden pegs to hold it together.

Despite a year-round stream of visitors, Woodstock has none of the garrishness that plagues many popular towns. In fact, it has fewer tourist accommodations than you might expect, and most of its visitors just pass through. Always reserved, urbane, and exclusive, Woodstock's appeal derives from the pristine charm of its homes and the tastefulness of its expensive shops. Four churches—the First Congregational (1807), St. James Episcopal (1907), the Universalist (1835), and the Masonic Temple, formerly Christian Church (1827)—still ring bells cast by Paul Revere.

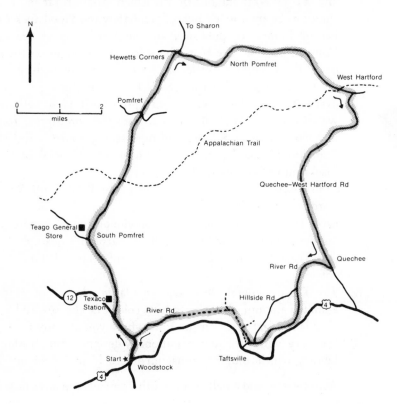

The Woodstock Historical Society, housed in the residence neurologist Charles L. Dana built for his family in 1807, exhibits a superior collection of early nineteenth-century antiques, including locally made furniture, portraits, silver, farm implements, quilts, doll houses, and etchings by John Taylor Arms. Behind the house an exquisitely landscaped garden stretches to the Ottauquechee. The Society is located at 26 Elm Street and open from Memorial Day through October, Monday through Saturday, 10:00 a.m. to 5:00 p.m., and Sunday, 2:00 p.m. to 5:30 p.m. Admission is $1.50 for adults and $.50 for children.

During the warm weather the town hosts many special events, including an antique automobile rally, a major AKC dog show, and several craft exhibits on the green. There is far more to see than can be mentioned here. Fortunately the Woodstock Chamber of Commerce publishes an annotated map of the village. You can get one free from the Information Booth on the green or at the Chamber's office at 4 Central Street. Before leaving town, you might also want to pick up some food, since little is available along the way. You can probably find something you would like at F. H. Gillingham & Sons (16 Elm Street), founded in 1886 as a general store and now selling gourmet foods; The Pumpkin House Natural Food Store (65a Central Street); or Blacksmith's Bakery (Mechanic Street).

1.0   At the Texaco station (on the right), bear RIGHT off Route 12 toward South Pomfret.

Over the next two miles the road climbs almost imperceptibly, but nevertheless steadily, as it follows Barnard Brook uphill.

3.0   At the Teago General Store in South Pomfret, bear RIGHT toward Pomfret.

The Teago General Store displays a large selection of wines and a limited amount of fresh produce, cold cuts, cheeses, and breads. This is the last place on the tour where you can buy food. Near the store stands the unconventionally designed Abbott Memorial Library, which contains a museum of local historical memorabilia.

About a mile and a half from South Pomfret, and later near West

Hartford, you cross the Appalachian Trail, which runs through southeastern Vermont on its way from Georgia to Maine.

South Pomfret sits at an elevation of 736' above sea level. Over the next three miles you climb nearly 500 feet—sometimes quite steeply—before reading Pomfret at 1,200'. This hill presents the only difficult ascent of the tour. From Pomfret you glide downhill seven miles to West Hartford, which lies at an elevation of 420' on the banks of the White River.

8.0 At Hewetts Corners, continue STRAIGHT. (Maps of the intersection at Hewetts Corners are deceptive. The road you follow through North Pomfret to West Hartford is a continuation of the road from Pomfret, while the road to Sharon branches off to your left. The maps make it appear as though the road to West Hartford requires a right turn in Hewetts Corners, but it does not.)

13.0 At the Stop Sign by the bridge outside West Hartford, turn RIGHT onto Quechee-West Hartford Road.

Off and on over the next three miles, the Quechee-West Hartford Road climbs gently out of the White River Valley. Then about two miles before the next turn, the road turns downhill.

18.0 One-tenth of a mile after the inverted Y road sign (on the right), turn sharply RIGHT onto River Road. Approach this turn cautiously, for when you reach it, you are going downhill.

Six-tenths of a mile after turning onto River Road, you pass the Quechee Club on the left. This modern clubhouse on the edge of a new golf course belongs to a major development of opulent condominiums and luxurious recreational facilities.

19.0 At the intersection where Hillside Road enters from your right, continue STRAIGHT on River Road.

20.8 At the second intersection of River Road and Hillside Road, continue STRAIGHT on River Road. (Your next turn comes in just one-tenth of a mile.)

20.9 Bear RIGHT onto Upper River Road, which is unpaved. (Trees may obscure the sign for this road, but it is easy to find since it is the first road on your right after the second intersection with Hillside Road.) From this turn to the next find your way simply by following the roads that keep the Ottauquechee River on your left.

Upper River Road is unpaved for two and three-tenths miles. While you could return to Woodstock on US 4, I do not recommend it because of the high volume of traffic, narrow road width, and lack of beauty. Although the unpaved road demands more than the usual amount of attention, it is quiet, shaded, and provides a delightful view of the Ottauquechee.

24.2 At the Stop Sign, turn LEFT onto Route 12 South.

24.5 You are back in Woodstock by the green where the tour began.

When you reach Woodstock, consider stretching your legs with a walk along one of the town's short nature trails: Faulkner Trail or Mount Peg Trail. Maps of both are available free from the Chamber of Commerce.

Bicycle Shops

Brown's Bike Shop, Bridge Street, White River Junction, VT   (802-295-7254)

The Brick Store, The Green, Strafford, VT   (802-765-6941)

The Cyclery Plus, US 4, West Woodstock, VT   (802-457-3377)

Rivers of Central Vermont:
A two-day tour

**The distance and terrain are stated at the beginning
of each day's directions.**

This tour offers not only fine rural bicycling, but exceptional opportunities to fish, swim, visit sites of historical and architectural interest, and view the state from the top of a mountain without having to cycle there. Along the way you may either camp or stay at country inns. Starting from Plymouth if you camp or Bridgewater Corners if you use inns, the route parallels rivers or streams nearly all the way. With the exception of twelve miles on US 4, which can be moderately busy, you follow lightly traveled roads—eight and a half miles of which are unpaved.

On the first day you visit the exquisite village of Woodstock, where the physical and spiritual flavor of early Vermont is carefully preserved. On the second you pass the Killington Gondola, which you can take to the top of Vermont's second highest mountain. And later that day you bicycle into the hill town of Plymouth, where Calvin Coolidge spent his boyhood and took his oath as president. Words Coolidge wrote about Plymouth nearly fifty years ago still fit that hamlet and most of the countryside along this route: "As I look back on it I constantly think how clean it was. There was little that was artificial. It was all close to nature and in accordance with the ways of nature. The streams ran clear. The roads, the woods, the fields, the people—all were clean. Even when I try to divest it of the halo which I know always surrounds the past, I am unable to create any other impression than that it was fresh and clean." (*Autobiography of Calvin Coolidge*, 1929.)

The tour is designed to suit both cyclists who like to camp and those who prefer to stay at country inns. Accordingly, two sets of mileages are given with the directions: campers' distances are indicated first and below them, in parentheses, are the mileages for cyclists traveling between inns. Regardless of which accommodations you use, you will probably find it convenient to sleep at the trail's head the night before you begin riding. If you camp, you will save time and eat better by bringing most of your food from home. But whichever way you go, do not set out until you have contacted the places you intend to stay at night, for you cannot rely on their being prepared for you without notice.

The inns on the tour are two of my favorite and have delighted many, many persons who have ridden with Vermont Bicycle Touring. Spend the night before you start cycling at Ruth and Pete Hall's October Country Inn. For a year Ruth led tours for Vermont Bicycle Touring, and she knows well the needs of bicyclists. She is one of the finest chefs in Vermont, and the consistently superb meals at the October Country Inn reflect her creative touch. Pete and Ruth have fashioned their cozy, cheerful inn from a nineteenth-century farmhouse. Informal, but gracious, the inn has no rooms with private baths and all guests eat at a single large table and bring their own liquor or do without. Though they run the inn virtually without help, Ruth and Pete and their dog Obadiah still manage to spend time with their guests and will surely make you feel that this lovely inn, which is their home, is yours too when you are there. Because they use the warm months to continue their remodeling of the building, the Halls do not always take guests during the bicycling season; so reservations are essential. The cost of lodging, dinner, breakfast, tax, and gratuity is approximately $20 per person. Make your reservations by contacting the Halls at October Country Inn, Box 66F, Bridgewater Corners, VT 05035 (802-672-3412). If you cannot be accommodated there, try the Salt Ash Inn, which is also lovely. Because it is located at the junction of Routes 100 and 100A—mileage 26.5 (26.0) on Day Two—

starting from Salt Ash lengthens your first day's ride by eight miles and shortens the second by the same distance. You can contact innkeepers Don and Ginny Kroitzsh at the Salt Ash Inn, Plymouth, VT 05056 (802-672-3748). They have a full liquor license, and their rates are about $11 per person, double occupancy, for a room, plus about $9 for breakfast and dinner, both of which require reservations. To these prices you should add 10 to 20 percent to cover the Vermont rooms and meals tax and gratuities.

For the night between Days One and Two, the tour goes to Tupper Farm Lodge. There is something magical about Tupper Farm, something that makes every guest feel wonderful but that cannot be fully explained even by its delicious, bountiful meals, comfortable accommodations, and superb swimming hole in the White River. It comes no doubt from the marvelous innkeepers Ann and Roger Verme, but it shall always remain their secret. Like their friends the Halls at October Country Inn, Ann and Roger have created their inn from an old farmhouse (1820). The wallpapered guest-rooms share baths; the lodge has no liquor license; and you can expect to join the other guests for a candlelit dinner at one large table. After a day's cycling Tupper Farm will immediately put you at ease. The magic will work, and you will know you have come to the right place. Rates, covering lodging, dinner, and breakfast, are about $20 per person, to which you should add 15 to 20 percent for tax and gratuity. You will need a reservation, which you make by contacting Tupper Farm Lodge, Box 43F, Rochester, VT 05767 (802-767-5461). If there is no space there, try the Stockbridge Inn, two and three-quarters miles south of Tupper Farm on Route 100—mileage (37.2) of Day One. Its rates and facilities are similar to Tupper Farm's. Innkeepers Bob and Leslie Skinner may be reached at The Stockbridge Inn, Stockbridge, VT 05772 (802-746-8165).

For campers the tour starts at Calvin Coolidge State Forest. Its season runs from the Friday before Memorial Day to mid-October. You may set up camp at one of twenty-five tent sites ($4.50 per night) or one of thirty-five three-sided, wooden floored, ten-by-thirteen-foot lean-tos ($5.50 per night). Vermont residents are charged $1.00 less. Some sites are in designated primitive areas accessible only by foot trail. Hot showers and flush toilets are provided. Vermont state parks do not accept reservations for fewer than six days; campsites are assigned on a first-come, first-served basis. For further information contact Calvin Coolidge State Forest, Plymouth, VT 05056 (802-672-3612).

Campers spend the night between Days One and Two at the White River Valley Camping Area, a member of VAPCOO. Owners Ginny and Denny Merrill have eighty wooded, open, and river sites that rent for $4.50 and up per night, and they gladly accept reservations for a single night. Flush toilets, hot showers, a laundromat, firewood, and ice as well as a small store selling mainly canned goods are available. For reservations contact the White River Valley Camping Area, Box 74, Gaysville, VT 05746 (802-234-9115)

Day One

Plymouth to Gaysville (Campgrounds): Moderate terrain; 36.5 miles
Bridgewater Corners to Rochester (Inns): Moderate terrain; 40 miles

0.0 At the exit from Calvin Coolidge State Forest turn RIGHT onto
—   Route 100A North.

Route 100A runs continuously downhill along Broad Brook for four miles and then flattens out a mile before Bridgewater Corners.

5.0 At the Stop Sign at Bridgewater Corners turn RIGHT onto US 4
(0.0) East. If you are starting from the October Country Inn, turn LEFT onto US 4 East.

At the intersection of US 4 and Route 100A, you can pick up supplies at the Junction Country Store. Owners Brenda and Lee Garsh have catered to the needs of bicyclists for many years and can help you quickly select some nourishment to carry as snacks. Their store features a broad selection of country wares as well as cheese, groceries, beverages, and penny candy. During the 1850s placer gold was discovered in Broad Brook above Bridgewater Corners. Something of a gold rush ensued, and there was a lot of panning and digging, but little gold turned up. Lee has tried a little panning himself and can probably be persuaded to tell you about it.

For the next eight miles you follow the Ottauquechee River, a good trout stream and, in the early spring, a challenging run for white-water canoeists. US 4 often draws a substantial amount of traffic, though it is not usually bothersome in the morning. Pay careful attention to your cycling, especially where the road is narrow. Five miles east of Bridgewater Corners you pass the Lincoln covered bridge, which stretches 136 feet across the Ottauquechee River. Constructed in 1865, this bridge remains Vermont's only example of a Pratt type truss.

13.0   At the intersection in the center of Woodstock, turn LEFT onto
(8.0)   Route 12 North.

Woodstock possesses more early nineteenth-century architectural grace than any town in Vermont and perhaps in New England. Stately public buildings and fine brick and clapboard townhouses, built one hundred fifty years ago, surround an unusual oval green. Woodstock has maintained its beauty and sustained its prosperity by pursuing finance and commerce, rather than manufacturing. Perhaps its former residents protected the village from change; certainly the current ones do. Telephone and electrical lines are buried; the exteriors of virtually all the buildings have been kept original; and in 1969, when another bridge was needed to cross the Ottauquechee, the town built an authentic covered bridge without a nail in it.

Woodstock draws visitors throughout the year, but only a few stay even overnight. In the evening the village belongs to its residents rather than tourists, because it offers little public entertainment. Steadfastly reserved, urbane, wealthy, and exclusive, Woodstock appeals to people of like qualities and in turn provides them with expensive shops, gracious clubs, and a village of the utmost visual charm. Four churches—the First Congregational (1807), St. James (1907), the Universalist (1835), and the Masonic Temple, formerly Christian Church (1827)— still ring bells cast by Paul Revere. You can probably acquire a better understanding of Woodstock in a brief time by visiting the Woodstock Historical Society than by doing anything else. In the elegant former residence (1807) of neurologist Charles L. Dana, the Society exhibits a fine collection of early nineteenth-century furnishings including portraits, silver, quilts, locally made furniture, doll houses, and farm implements as well as old historical records and etchings by John Taylor Arms. Behind the house beautiful gardens lead down to the Ottauquechee. The Society is located at 26 Elm Street and open from Memorial Day through October, Monday through Saturday, 10:00 a.m. to 5:00 p.m., and Sunday, 2:00 p.m. to 5:30 p.m. Admission is $1.50 for adults and $.50 for children.

During Vermont's warm months Woodstock produces many special events, including an antique automobile rally, a major AKC dog show, and several art and craft exhibits. Information about these and other events can be obtained from the Woodstock Chamber of Commerce, which also publishes an annotated map of the village. You may get a map free at the information booth on the green or the Chamber's office at 4 Central Street.

About four miles north of Woodstock you pass a state historical sign marking a spot of enormous significance to Vermont. In 1934, on a hilly sheep pasture here, two ingenious Yankees hitched a rope to the engine of a Model T Ford to create the first ski tow in America. Now more than forty ski areas operate in Vermont alone, accommodating in a single season seven times the state's population. Just beyond the site of the tow, you cross the Appalachian Trail, which runs from Maine to Georgia. Route 12 then turns uphill, presenting a long and sometimes arduous climb. A level respite of a half-mile divides the winding grade into two parts, each a mile and three-quarters long. The first ascent remains gradual; the second, ending by a room-sized quartz boulder on the right, starts gently, but quickly grows steep. Over the four miles you gain roughly 850' in elevation. But with that climb you complete all the hard work of the day and descend rapidly two miles into Barnard.

23.0   At Barnard, do not curve left to follow Route 12 North; instead
(18.0) go STRAIGHT off Route 12 onto North Road.

Barnard makes an ideal place to picnic. The Barnard General
Store stocks an ample selection of food and also runs a lunch
counter where you can get hot soup and cooked meals. Across
from the store, a lawn by the shore of Silver Lake provides a
perfect place to stretch out, have lunch, and enter the clear
waters for a swim. If you are headed for the campground, the
Barnard Store is a reliable place to get supplies, and, if you are
bound for Tupper Farm Lodge, you can pick up beer or wine.
During the 1930s Sinclair Lewis and Dorothy Thompson lived
in Barnard, and Thompson is buried in the cemetery here.

North Road runs past the southern tip of Silver Lake, up a short,
gentle hill, and then along a plateau from which you can catch
glimpses of the Green Mountains to your left. About three miles
from Barnard, the road begins to tilt downward, getting progressively steeper as it approaches Bethel. The last mile and a
half are very fast and require your complete attention; by the
time you reach Bethel you have descended over 700'. Three
and three-quarters miles from Barnard, North Road becomes
unpaved for a mile just after passing a lumber yard on the right.
The road is well packed and generally free of rocks but should be
ridden cautiously, since some of it goes downhill.

29.8   At the Stop Sign outside Bethel, turn RIGHT onto Route 107 East.
(24.8) Bethel was the first town chartered by the Republic of Vermont
during its fourteen years as an independent nation, 1777-91.
The route does not go into the village, and there is no reason to
ride there unless you need supplies.

30.5   After crossing a bridge and just before Route 12 goes beneath an
(25.5) underpass, turn LEFT onto the very small, unsigned road.

In a mile and a half this road becomes unpaved for four miles.
The surface remains hard and smooth for three miles, but becomes slightly soft near the end, when you must climb a half-
mile hill.

34.8   At the fork, where the road is still unpaved, bear LEFT so you
(29.8) cross a very small bridge.

36.3   One-half mile after the pavement resumes, at the bottom of a short
(31.3)   hill, turn LEFT and cross the green iron bridge into Gaysville,
             which consists only of a church and tiny post office.

The day's second superb swimming spot lies directly below this
bridge in the White River. One of the principal tributaries of
the Connecticut River, the White runs approximately sixty
miles from Battell Mountain (el. 3471'), west of Granville, to
White River Junction. Its wonderfully clean waters provide not
only exceptional swimming, but fine cover for trout—especially
rainbows and browns—and excellent, though strenuous, white-
water canoeing.

36.5   The driveway to the White River Valley Camping area, the end of
(31.5)   the day's ride for campers, begins on your left immediately after
             the green bridge.

—   At the T just beyond the Gaysville post office (on the left), turn
(31.6)   RIGHT onto Route 107 West.

In three miles Route 107 runs gradually uphill for three-quarters
of a mile.

—   At the intersection of Routes 107 and 100, turn RIGHT onto
(36.0)   Route 100 North.

—   At the blinker in Stockbridge, which is simply a crossroad, turn
(37.2)   LEFT to continue north on Route 100.

When you reach this blinker, you are facing The Stockbridge
Inn.

—   Tupper Farm Lodge stands on your right facing Route 100, six
(40.0)   miles south of the village of Rochester.

Day Two

Gaysville to Plymouth (Campgrounds): Moderate terrain; 29.5 miles
Rochester to Bridgewater Corners (Inns): Moderate terrain; 34.5 miles

0.0   From White River Valley Camping Area, turn LEFT out of the
—   driveway onto the unsigned road.
0.1   At the T just beyond the Gaysville post office (on the left), turn
—   RIGHT onto Route 107 West.

In three miles Route 107 runs up a gradual hill for three-quarters of a mile.

—
(0.0)
From Tupper Farm Lodge, turn LEFT onto Route 100 South.

—
(2.8)
At the blinker in Stockbridge, turn RIGHT to continue south on Route 100.

4.5
(4.0)
At the intersection of Routes 107 and 100, go STRAIGHT onto Route 100 South.

On a clear day when no nearby hills obstruct your view, you can see the top of Killington Peak directly ahead of you. In a mile and a half you pass the Pittsfield Potters on your right. They are open daily from 9:00 a.m. to 5:00 p.m., and you can often watch the pottery being made. Four miles south of the village of Pittsfield you begin climbing a moderate, but relentless, grade which in two miles takes you 550' up in elevation.

13.5
(13.0)
One-half mile past the sign (on the right) for Trailside Lodge and just where a yellow and black arrow directs traffic on Route 100 to the right, turn LEFT off Route 100 onto River Road, which is unpaved for the first three and a half miles.

The surface of River Road is hard, smooth, and generally free of rocks, but ride very cautiously on the sections that go downhill.

17.5
(17.0)
At the Stop Sign in Sherburne Center (Killington P.O.), turn LEFT onto Route 100 South, which here runs concurrently with US 4 East.

Over the next four miles you encounter more traffic than you have seen since leaving Woodstock yesterday. However the road is wide, straight, and offers a shoulder suitable for cycling most of the way.

In two miles, at the end of Sherburne flats, you reach the Killington Gondola Tramway, the world's longest ski lift. The three-and-a-half-mile-long ride is exciting and certainly worth while on a clear day. The views from the top are no less than spectacular, and you can enjoy them while having lunch at the Peak Restaurant.

If you can, take along a map to orient yourself and help you identify the major geological formations you can see in five states: Vermont, Maine, New Hampshire, New York, and Massachusetts. From the gondola you can walk along a short trail to the top of Killington Peak (el. 4,235'), Vermont's second tallest mountain. The tramway operates daily from mid-June to late October between 10:30 a.m. and 4:45 p.m.; on Wednesday through Sunday evenings it also makes sunset trips. Round-trip rates are $4.50 for adults, $2.25 for children from six to twelve, and free for those younger. Shortly past the gondola, Route 100 dives downhill for a mile into West Bridgewater.

21.5   At the blinker in West Bridgewater, turn RIGHT onto Route 100 **(21.0)**   South.

Jim & Zel's Corner Store, to your right at this intersection, makes good fresh sandwiches and sells all you need for a fine picnic. A half-mile south of the store, Route 100 starts up a gradual grade that grows steeper before ending in a mile and a half at the foot of Woodward Reservoir. A tenth of a mile after you draw alongside the reservoir, you can see a turn-out for cars and a broad lawn where you can picnic and swim.

26.5   In Plymouth Union, by the Salt Ash Inn on your left, turn LEFT **(26.0)**   onto Route 100A.

Immediately upon making this turn, you face one of Vermont's most formidable short ascents. Fondly and not-so-fondly called Hysteria Hill by many bicyclists, this climb, though barely a half-mile long, tests the stamina and will of all who try it. But doubtless it merits the effort, for it brings an unspoiled down-hill run of more than five miles. Of course, if you began this tour at Calvin Coolidge State Forest, you benefited from four of those miles yesterday.

27.5   Four-tenths of a mile beyond the crest of Hysteria Hill and just past **(27.0)**   a pond on your right, turn LEFT off Route 100A onto the road toward Plymouth and ride a half-mile to that village.

Plymouth deserves a visit for both aesthetic and historical reasons. Consisting only of a few trim nineteenth-century clapboard buildings and surrounded by hills, this tiny hamlet radiates peacefulness and security. Here, at three o'clock on an August morning in 1923, Vice-president Calvin Coolidge was awakened to be told that President Harding had died. Then, by the glow of a kerosene lamp, the most modern form of lighting in the house, Coolidge took the presidential oath from his father, a notary public. Fifty-one years earlier on Independence Day Coolidge was born here in a weathered cottage beside the church where his family worshipped.

The cottage where Calvin Coolidge was born, from the window of the Union Christian Church

Now a state historic site, Plymouth merits a leisurely visit. The Coolidge family home, where the vice-president was vacationing when Harding died, has been painstakingly restored to its condition on that eventful night. In like manner the room where Coolidge was born has been refurbished as the nineteenth-century borning room that it was. Along with the Wilder House, where the president's mother lived until she married, these buildings accurately portray a style of life common in Vermont nearly a century ago. Still more can be learned about those times by visiting the immense old barn that now houses the Vermont Farmers Museum. Its collection of hand-wrought farm implements dramatically illustrates the hardship farm families endured and the ingenious ways they accomplished with animal and human power tasks now performed by electricity and internal combustion engines. From late May till mid-October these buildings are open to the public daily between 9:30 a.m. and 5:30 p.m. Admission is $1 for adults and free for children thirteen and younger.

Plymouth's Union Christian Church (1840), originally Congregational, illustrates the blending of mid- and late-nineteenth century architecture. The exterior remains unchanged since its construction and resembles that of many other clapboard meetinghouses around the state. But in 1890 the congregation decided to replace the original box pews with a more up-to-date arrangement. Accordingly they hired a master carpenter who refashioned the interior out of rare hard pine in a style known as Carpenter Gothic. This style achieves in wood the Gothic forms usually shaped by masonry. The church holds services during July and August at 11:00 a.m. on Sundays. The Calvin Coolidge Memorial Center (1972) houses an interesting collection of Coolidge memorabilia, including many old photographs captioned with excerpts from his autobiography. Finally, the Plymouth Cheese Corporation at the northern end of the village makes Plymouth's unique curd cheese. On weekdays you can watch the process, and every day of the week you can sample the cheese and buy it.

28.5 Retrace your way out of Plymouth and turn LEFT onto Route 100A
(28.0) toward Woodstock.

29.5 The entrance to Calvin Coolidge State Forest is on your right,
(29.0) where, if you have been camping, you started this tour.

— At the Stop Sign in Bridgewater Corners, turn LEFT onto US 4,
(34.0) ride two tenths of a mile, and turn RIGHT toward Bridgewater
Center. Go fifty yards, turn RIGHT onto the unpaved road, and
ride another one hundred fifty yards to the October Country
Inn, where you started the tour.

Bicycle Shops

Brown's Bike Shop, Bridge Street, White River Junction, VT   (802-295-7254)

Green Mountain Schwinn Cyclery, 133 Strongs Avenue, Rutland, VT
(802-775-0869)

Sports Peddler, 162 North Main Street (US 7), Rutland, VT   (802-775-0182)

The Brick Store, The Green, Strafford, VT   (802-765-6941)

The Cyclery Plus, US 4, West Woodstock, VT   (802-457-3377)

South Royalton-Strafford

Moderate terrain; 29 miles

With the exception of the Northeast Kingdom, fifty to seventy-five miles further north, Orange County may be Vermont's most unspoiled region. It has no ski areas, no major lakes, no cities, and no major mountains. Even Vermont's two Interstate highways, 89 and 91, which enclose this unheralded county on the south, east, and west, seem to funnel the traffic by. And yet Orange County is a wonderland of wooded hills and narrow river valleys, ideal for bicycling. This tour begins in the village of South Royalton and follows untrafficked roads along the First and West Branches of the White River as well as the White River itself. Carving an undulating circle through the tiny villages of South Strafford, Strafford, and Tunbridge, the tour brings excellent views down the valleys and across the rounded hills that feed their streams into the rivers below. Though the route is emphatically pastoral, you have opportunities to visit three covered bridges, an interesting craft gallery, and the magnificent mid-nineteenth-century home of Justin Morrill. And, if you make the tour in mid-September, you can complete the day by joining the spirited whirl of the Tunbridge World's Fair.

0.0   Leave South Royalton by riding east on South Windsor Street, the unsigned road running along the northern side of the green.

The recently founded Vermont Law School, the state's first, stands near the green in an old elementary school. A private, three-year institution, the law school enrolls approximately 350 men and women. In Vermont aspiring lawyers may also gain admission to the bar by reading law with a practicing attorney and then taking the state bar examination. The Royalton Historical Society Museum, located in the 1840 Town House, contains articles relating to the 1780 Indian raid on Royalton and Tunbridge and to the former Bank of Royalton as well as photographs, broadsides, maps, and other possessions of the town's early residents. The museum opens on the first and third Saturdays of July and August and by appointment (802-763-8830). During the summer on Friday evenings the South Royalton Town Band performs on the green. South Windsor Street parallels the White River, which along this stretch offers good swimming and excellent fishing for brown and rainbow trout. Three miles from town, the street tips slightly downward for a mile, which ends as you pass beneath Interstate 89.

4.6 Follow South Windsor Street around a ninety-degree left curve and across an iron bridge.

4.7 At the Stop Sign outside Sharon, turn RIGHT onto Route 14 East.

5.0 Just after passing Brooksie's Diner (on the left) in Sharon, turn LEFT onto Route 132 East.

Joseph Smith, founder of the Church of Jesus Christ of Latter-Day Saints, the Mormons, was born on an outlying Sharon farm in 1805. Smith lived there till he was ten and received his first visitation four years later in New York. About five miles from this intersection, at the end of a two-mile climb up an unpaved road, a quiet retreat has been built at Smith's birthplace. A monolith of Barre granite, 38½ feet high and weighing thirty-nine tons—purportedly the world's largest—marks the site. Each foot of the obelisk represents a year in the life of the prophet, who was lynched by a mob in the Carthage, Illinois, jail in 1844. Had it not been for the organizational genius of another Vermonter, Brigham Young, who was born in Whitingham, Mormonism might have died with Smith.

Within a quarter-mile Route 132 rolls moderately uphill for a mile and a quarter, down for three-quarters, and then up again for a mile. After following a plateau three-quarters of a mile, you start down a glorious two-mile descent. Initially the slope is extremely steep so take it cautiously and enjoy the views.

11.6   At the Stop Sign in South Strafford, turn LEFT off Route 132 toward Strafford.

If you want groceries, which are not available again until Tunbridge, turn RIGHT instead of left at this Stop Sign and ride two hundred yards to Coburns' General Store. For seven miles from South Strafford you follow the West Branch of the White River.

In three miles you reach Strafford, where problems with your bicycle can be remedied at The Brick Store, a bicycle shop open from 10:00 a.m. to 6:00 p.m., Tuesday through Saturday.

You might also enjoy pausing in Strafford to visit the American Gothic homestead Justin S. Morrill had built for himself from 1848 to 1851. Now a state historic site and National Register Property, the brick and stone building is open daily except Mondays from late May until mid-October. Morrill, who represented Vermont in the U.S. House and Senate for forty-three years, was born in Strafford. He is known best for the Morrill Act passed during the Civil War. It granted each loyal state federal land for the support of colleges that would teach agriculture and the mechanic arts. Under this act and its successors states received 17,400,000 acres of land—nearly three times the area of Vermont—and by 1961 sixty-nine land-grant colleges had been established. The Morrill Act brought about the first major practical and technical programs of study in American higher education, previously the exclusive bastion of classical studies in arts and sciences.

The white meetinghouse that stands on a hill in the center of Strafford was built in 1799 and is reputed to be the oldest Universalist Church in the country. On the green near The Brick Store the Vermont Artisans Gallery, a craft cooperative, displays and sells works of central Vermont craftspeople. The Gallery also presents special exhibitions and chamber music concerts. In the same building the Stone Soup Restaurant serves homemade lunches from noon to 2:00 p.m., Wednesday through Saturday.

Just beyond Strafford you start up a gradual but steady grade that reaches the crest of the tour's last climb in slightly over four miles. Trees shade the road most of the way, but you still have a fine view of the surrounding hills from the top. Then the road drops steeply into a fast three-and-a-half-mile run into Tunbridge.

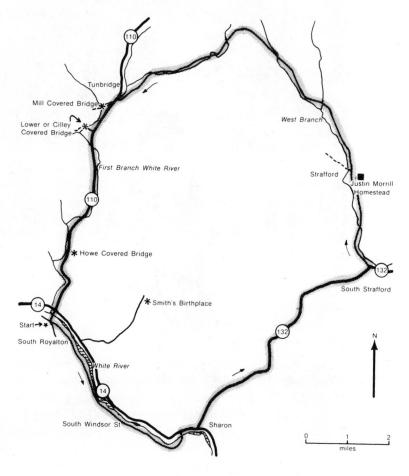

Up one of the tour's numerous hills

21.7 At the Stop Sign in Tunbridge, turn LEFT onto Route 110 South.

For over a century Tunbridge has been celebrating the World's Fair of the Union Agricultural Society here in mid-September. Sometimes drawing 15,000 persons in a day, the four-day festival blends the exuberant spirit of a carnival with the exhibits and competitions of an agricultural fair. Folklore says that in years past all sober persons were herded off the grounds at three in the afternoon as undesirables. Others say the bacchanalian tradition continues. In any case, if you arrive during the fair, judge for yourself and watch the traffic carefully. Information about the official events can be obtained from the Town Clerk, Tunbridge, VT 05077 (802-889-5521).

Within a tenth of a mile after you start south on Route 110, you can see the Mill covered bridge. Built across the First Branch of the White River in 1883, its structure is Multiple Kingpost, having a span of sixty feet. Just beyond the bridge, you can get groceries at the Tunbridge Village Store. A mile further south, if you turn off Route 110 onto the unpaved road which enters from the west, you can find the Lower or Cilley covered bridge. This bridge, also built in 1883, measures sixty-five feet. Three miles later, the sixty-foot Howe covered bridge, built in 1879, comes into view on your left. Route 110 slopes slightly downward nearly the entire way, as it follows the First Branch of the White River seven miles to South Royalton.

28.7 At the Stop Sign at the intersection of Routes 110 and 14, go STRAIGHT across Route 14 onto the road to South Royalton.

29.0 You enter South Royalton along the west side of the green, where the tour began.

Bicycle Shops

Brown's Bicycle Shop, Bridge Street, White River Junction, VT (802-295-7254)

The Brick Store, The Green, Strafford, VT (802-765-6941)

The Cyclery Plus, US 4, West Woodstock, VT (802-457-3377)

10

Waitsfield-Warren

Easy-to-moderate terrain; 16 miles

The Waitsfield-Warren area, known as the Sugarbush* or Mad
River Valley, offers some fine cycling amidst the attractions of one
of the East's finest ski resorts. Starting a half-mile south of Waitsfield, this tour visits two charming villages, each with its own
covered bridge, and then explores open, generally level countryside
at the base of the Lincoln range of the Green Mountains. Recreation has largely displaced farming and lumbering as the principal
business of the Valley, and consequently you can combine this short
bicycle tour with other activity, such as a glider or balloon ride out
of the Warren airport (802-496-3148), horseback riding at any of
several stables, tennis at many inns and hotels, golf at the Robert
Trent golf course, or trout fishing in the Mad River. If you prefer
something less strenuous, you can watch polo matches on Sundays
at 2:00 p.m. in Waitsfield or Warren or rugby matches at the same
time on Saturdays at the Waitsfield Recreation Area. And the
numerous shops and restaurants along Route 100 at the tour's con-
clusion will surely satisfy the appetites of the most curious shopper
or hungry gourmet. The tour begins at the Mad River Green
Shopping Center midway between Irasville and Waitsfield on the
northwest side of Route 100, a half-mile north of the intersection
of Routes 100 and 17.

*Sugarbush is a generic term for any woods of sugar maple trees. The word derives
from the time when sap was collected and boiled to make sugar, rather than syrup.
The process, which takes place in the early spring, is still called sugaring whether
its product is syrup or sugar. The valley and one of its ski areas have taken their names
from the stands of sugar maples on Lincoln Peak and the neighboring hills.

0.0   Turn LEFT out of the Mad River Green Shopping Center onto
Route 100 North.

Before leaving the shopping center, you might stop at The
Breadbasket Bakery to choose some freshly made bread and
pastry, cheese, delicatessen cold cuts, or other treats to carry
along.

Barely after you have shifted gears for the first time, you reach
the Village Square Shopping Center on your right. Stop there
at the Information Booth to get a copy of *The Valley Reporter's*
free fifty-six-page pamphlet, "The Mad River Valley Vermont."

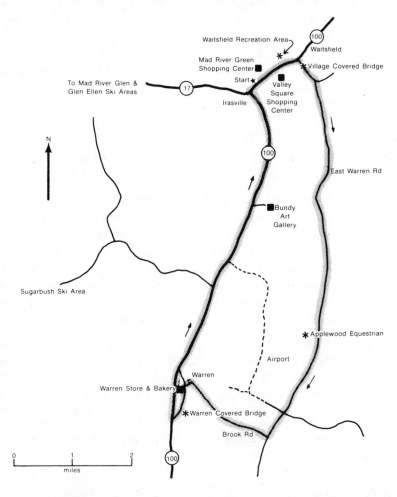

It provides a wealth of useful information about the natural, recreational, and commercial life of the area. And while you are there, inquire about special events that might be happening along the route, such as concerts, craft exhibits, fairs, and sporting contests. Should you want further information or wish to make reservations anywhere closeby, take advantage of the hospitality of the tiny Waitsfield-Fayston Telephone Company. You can make local calls free from the public telephones in each of the Waitsfield and Irasville shopping centers as well as in the villages of Waitsfield and Warren. The Cheese Shop in the Village Square purveys a broad selection of local and imported cheeses as well as crackers, wines, and sweets—all of which will taste especially good when you reach the top of the hill outside Waitsfield.

0.8 Opposite the Troll Shop (on the left) in Waitsfield, turn RIGHT onto East Warren Road. (There may not be a street sign at this intersection, but you are on course if you cross a covered bridge within a quarter-mile.)

The Troll Shop, built in 1817, is the oldest surviving residence in Waitsfield. It is now a clothing store. The Village or Big Eddy covered bridge reaches 113 feet over the Mad River. It was built in 1833 and recently restored by Milton Grafton and Sons.

Just beyond the bridge, East Warren Road begins an ascent that is nearly two and a half miles long. The grade is steady but seldom steep, and it is the only trying climb of the tour.

1.2 At the fork, continue STRAIGHT uphill toward East Warren.

In about a mile and a half, just as the hill ends, the rare and handsome Joslin round barn rises on your left. Constructed in 1910, it is the last round barn left in the Mad River Valley and one of only a few still standing in Vermont.

Three and a half miles past the barn, you come to the Applewood Equestrian Center. On alternate Sundays polo matches are held here at 2:00 p.m. If you make arrangements ahead of time (802-496-2162), you can temporarily switch steeds and take a horseback ride—either English or Western style.

Three-quarters of a mile past the stables, the road turns downhill, making a fast, exhilarating descent for two and a half miles into Warren.

7.0 At the crossroad, go STRAIGHT to continue on East Warren Road. Off to the west (on your right), the trails of the Sugarbush Ski Area stand out clearly on the wooded slopes of Lincoln Peak (el. 3,975').

7.5 Follow the main road as it curves ninety degrees to the right. (On some maps the road changes name at this point to Brook Road; but in any case there is no street sign.)

The descent gets progressively steeper as you approach Warren. So heed the road signs and ride the last half-mile slowly.

9.3 At the Yield Sign in Warren, turn LEFT onto the unsigned road.

In a hundred yards you reach the Warren Store and Bakery on your right. Located in a former inn and library with the village post office in back, the store stocks an attractive variety of foods, which make it a favorite stopping place for cyclists. The breads are excellent as are the wines. And large wooden bins are heaped high with dried fruits, nuts, penny candy, and fresh produce. The balcony upstairs has been made into a country boutique selling clothing, fabrics, baskets, and kitchenwares.

While you are at the store, get directions to the dam and old abandoned lumber mills south of the village on the Mad River. Until the surrounding area became a downhill skiing center, Warren was a lumber milling town. Just below the dam, where the Mad River cuts through a rocky, jagged gorge, it has carved a natural bridge of stone, called The Arch. If you feel like stretching your legs a with a short hike, ask the shopkeepers to point out the way to the mile-long trail leading up Lincoln Brook from the bobbin mill.

As you leave Warren, stop again to look at the Warren covered bridge that Walter Bagley built in 1880 and at the waterfalls below it. Calm and clear above the falls, the Mad River makes excellent swimming here.

10.0 At the Stop Sign, turn RIGHT onto Route 100 North.

The main artery of the Sugarbush Valley, Route 100 connects

Cycling by a pasture near Warren

Warren to Waitsfield and feeds traffic to the valley's three ski areas—Glen Ellen, Mad River Glen, and Sugarbush—and to the summer recreational facilities that have sprung up near them. Consequently the traffic can get heavy, especially in the afternoon and during July, August, and early October. Nevertheless the road provides safe cycling amidst a mixture of visitors' attractions and rural scenes. Furthermore it is nearly flat.

In about three miles, you find the driveway to the Bundy Art Gallery by looking carefully for its sign on your right just after you cross a bridge. The gallery, actually a museum, is housed in a contemporary building on eighty acres of woods and fields at the end of a half-mile, uphill, unpaved drive and definitely merits a visit. Large metal and wooden outdoor sculptures sit dramatically in a serene natural setting, enhanced by open spaces cleared from the woods and a man-made duck pond that reflects the mountains in its surface. Inside the museum paintings and more sculpture by Vermont artists and others are on display. On many Sunday afternoons in July and August, the Bundy presents free outdoor concerts. It is open from July through Labor Day from 10:00 a.m. to 5:00 p.m., except on Sundays when the hours are 1:00 p.m. to 5:00 p.m. and on Tuesdays when it is closed. Admission is free. For scheduling information, call 802-496-3713.

Over the last half-mile of the tour—from the intersection of Routes 100 and 17 north to the Mad River Green Shopping Center—both sides of the road offer an interesting assortment of eateries, shops, and galleries. It would be easy to spend a pleasant afternoon exploring these places and sampling their wares.

16.0 The Mad River Green Shopping Center, where you began, is on the left.

Bicycle Shops

Demers Repair, Inc., 81 South Main Street, Barre, VT   (802-476-7712)

Inverness Ski and Sports, Mad River Green Shopping Center, Waitsfield, VT (802-496-3343)

Onion River Sports, 20 Langdon Street, Montpelier, VT   (802-229-9409)

11

Brandon-Fort Ticonderoga

Moderate-to-difficult terrain; 44 miles

This route highlights Revolutionary history, apple orchards, fertile dairylands, and panoramic vistas in the southern Champlain Valley, "Land of Milk and Honey." To maximize the superlative long views of the Adirondack and Green mountains it is best to ride the route on a clear day. Leaving Brandon and then twice crossing the Otter Creek, an important Indian waterway two hundred years ago, you cycle parts of the old Crown Point Military Road, which Lord Jeffrey Amherst cut through the wilderness from Charlestown, New Hampshire, to Lake Champlain in 1759. It was this road that Colonel Henry Knox and his army of farmers used during the winter of 1775 to haul fifty-nine cannons overland from Fort Ticonderoga to Boston, where they played a critical role in expelling the British. The tour merits its moderate to difficult rating, because the ride back to Brandon from Fort Ticonderoga is hilly and considerably more demanding than the ride out.

0.0   From the Brandon green ride north on US 7.

US 7 is narrow and heavily traveled in this vicinity.

Brandon was chartered in 1761, and fine post-Revolutionary and Victorian homes line its wide streets. Stephan A. Douglas, "The Little Giant" who opposed Abraham Lincoln for the presidency in 1860, was born here in 1813. The story-and-a-half cottage that was his birthplace sits at the northern end of the village, on your left as you leave town on US 7. The cottage now serves the local Daughters of the American Revolution as their headquarters and is open to the public on Thursday afternoons from 2:00 p.m. to 5:00 p.m., June through September. Firmly Republican in 1860, Brandon voted for Lincoln rather than its native son. Currently during the summer, the Brandon Inn, which stands opposite the green at the center of the village, offers dinner theater under the direction of the Brandon Arts Council.

1.5 At the Pine Hill Cemetery (on the right), turn LEFT onto the unsigned road that runs northwest off US 7 past the Brandon Training School, which is visible on your left. (No sign may be in evidence at the cemetery, but it is the only cemetery in this vicinity.)

4.5 At the small sign (on the right) for Whiting, turn LEFT onto the unsigned road toward Whiting.

8.5   At the Stop Sign in Whiting, go STRAIGHT across Route 30 onto the unsigned road.

The Corner Cupboard on the left side of this intersection is the last place you can buy food until you reach Shoreham six and a half miles away. In May, 1775, when Ethan Allen wanted to gather the Green Mountain Boys for their famous attack on Fort Ticonderoga, he dispatched Whiting blacksmith Samuel Beach as his messenger. The hearty Vermonter ran sixty-four miles in twenty-four hours to summon the backwoods clan for its sally across Lake Champlain.

14.5   At the Stop Sign, turn RIGHT onto Route 22A North.

15.0   At Herb's Corner Store (on the left) in Shoreham, turn LEFT onto Route 74 West.

The Shop at the Shoreham Inn, on the right side of Route 74 a

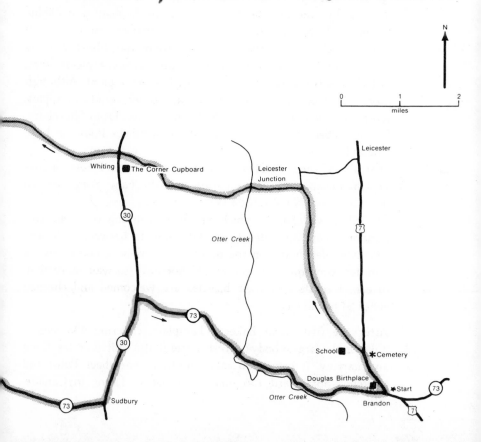

The panoramic views on this tour resemble those near Jay Peak

quarter-mile beyond Herb's, sells an assortment of delicious food and drink and treats bicyclists with great affection. A quarter-mile further on, also on the right, is the Lapham and Dibble Gallery, which restores and sells fine American paintings and prints. Cyclists are always welcome there too. Shoreham sits at the heart of Addison County's prosperous apple-growing district and features a cooperative apple storage plant. Although more McIntosh are harvested than any other variety of apples, scores of kinds are grown in Addison County. From Shoreham, Route 74 begins a gradual descent to Larrabees Point on Lake Champlain.

20.0 At Larrabees Point, STOP to take the tiny Shorewell Ferry across Lake Champlain. After disembarking on the New York side, go STRAIGHT onto NY Route 74 West.

The Shorewell Ferry, which has been running for over two hundred years, operates from 8:00 a.m. to between 5:30 and 9:00 p.m., depending on the month. The crossing takes only six minutes; consequently you should not have to wait more than fifteen. Cyclists and their bicycles are welcomed and charged about $1 round trip.

After the five Great Lakes, Champlain, covering 435 square miles, is the largest body of fresh water in the United States. Long and narrow, it begins 35 miles south of Larrabees Point and stretches northward 136 miles, the last 18 falling in Canada.

At its widest point, north of Burlington, the lake measures 15 miles, but most of it is much narrower. In winter it freezes to an average depth of twenty-two inches—enough to support cars and light trucks as well as ice fishermen. Champlain is one of few lakes in North America that flows north, emptying into the Saint Lawrence River. A series of twelve locks near Whitehall, New York, connects the lake at its southern end to the Hudson River. The swimming at Larrabees Point is not attractive, because this part of the lake has been badly polluted by the International Paper Company of Ticonderoga, New York.

The section of NY Route 74 which leads to Fort Ticonderoga is nearly all uphill.

20.5   At the sign for Fort Ticonderoga, turn LEFT and follow the mile-long driveway to the fort. After your visit, retrace your way back to the ferry and return to Vermont.

Between mid-May and mid-October visitors are welcome at Fort Ticonderoga from 8:00 a.m. to 6:00 p.m. Admission to the fort and its fine military museum is well worth the $3 charged adults and $1.50 charged children ages ten to thirteen. Younger children are admitted free. A restaurant, gift shop, and large pleasant picnic area are located outside the stockade and are available without charge. The descendants of William Ferris Pell, who purchased the fort in ruins in 1820, have restored it magnificently. Now a National Historic Landmark, Fort Ticonderoga is still owned and managed by the Pell family. A fife and drum corps regularly performs outside the fort.

Militarily, the fort was key to Lake Champlain and served in turn the French, who built it, the British, the Revolutionary colonists, and the United States. Symbolically it has long been a monument to the audacity of Ethan Allen and his eighty-three Green Mountain Boys, who captured it from the sleeping British commander La Place in the morning darkness of May 10, 1775. Although their triumph was due to surprise rather than military force, it nevertheless greatly buoyed the spirits of the Revolutionary troops.

23.0   From the ferry landing at Larrabees Point, go STRAIGHT onto Route 74 East.

23.6   Turn RIGHT onto Route 73 East and follow its twists and turns through Orwell and Sudbury all the way back to Brandon.

It is this portion of the route—the sixteen miles from Larrabees Point to the Otter Creek, three miles west of Brandon—that makes the tour more demanding than moderate cycling. Route 73 mounts several hills, some steep and some long. These climbs are relieved by stretches of level riding and an occasional downhill run, but the ride is difficult because it also makes up in elevation the 450-foot difference in height between Brandon and Lake Champlain.

Orwell is the last place you can buy food or drink until you reach Brandon, fourteen miles away. During the middle of the nineteenth century, Orwell became prosperous as a center of Vermont's vigorous wool industry. In the 1830s Merino sheep were the state's principal livestock, and most of the state was cleared for their pasture. Though sheep raising faded in Vermont after the Civil War, it is now enjoying a revival.

The Otter Creek makes poor swimming. At seventy-five miles the state's longest river, it flows lazily northward from Mount Tabor Town to Vergennes, where it empties into Lake Champlain. Along the way it gathers the runoff of thousands of acres of pastureland as well as some insufficiently treated industrial and residential waste.

43.6   At the Yield Sign, turn RIGHT onto US 7 South.

44.0   You are back in Brandon where the tour began.

Bicycle Shops

Bike & Ski Touring Center, 22 Main Street, Middlebury, VT   (802-388-6666)

Green Mountain Schwinn Cyclery, 133 Strongs Avenue, Rutland, VT (802-775-0869)

Skihaus Mountain Sports, 56 Main Street, Middlebury, VT   (802-388-2823)

Sports Peddler, 162 North Main Street (US 7), Rutland, VT   (802-775-0182)

Vermont Bicycle Touring, Munger Street, New Haven, VT   (802-388-4011)

12

Middlebury-Vergennes

Easy terrain; 51 miles

Starting from the extraordinary college town and crafts center of Middlebury, this tour explores the historic Champlain Valley. Here in Addison County, flat and fertile farmlands nestling between the Green and Adirondack mountains provide some of the most panoramic views in Vermont. Fragrant apple orchards, rustling cornfields, and peaceful farms line the roads. Level except for a mile and a half climb near the end, this tour provides an excellent opportunity to ride a Half-century in Vermont. (A Half-century is a bicycling standard established by the League of American Wheelmen whereby a cyclist must complete 50 miles in an elapsed, not riding, time of six hours or less. To ride a Century one must cover 100 miles in twelve hours; a Double Century, 200 in twenty-four.)

The route takes you through the campus of Middlebury College, along the shore of Lake Champlain, and near the sites of several important battles of the Revolution and War of 1812. The ride closes with a stop at the University of Vermont's Morgan Horse Farm and passage through one of only six remaining two-lane covered bridges in the United States. Start your ride at Jane and Frank Emanuel's charming Middlebury Inn (1827), which treats bicyclists with the greatest hospitality and serves a delicious buffet dinner, generous enough to satisfy the appetites of the most ravenous riders.

0.0   From the Middlebury Inn follow Route 125 West toward Bridport.

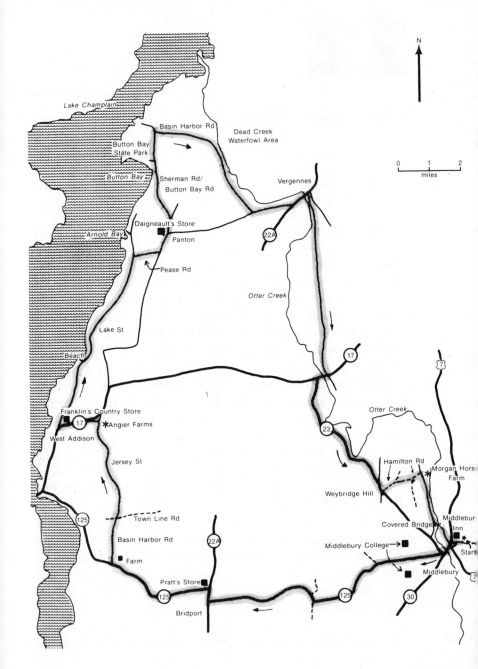

Described in *A Walking History of Middlebury* by art historian Glenn M. Andres as a town that "has remained to a remarkable degree the village that the eighteenth and nineteenth centuries built," Middlebury is not merely of local architectural interest. According to Andres, its buildings document a "progression from frontier community to manufacturing center, to agricultural center, to local service center . . . [and] can be taken as representative as well of almost every major style of American building from the colonial period onward."

At the center of town in Frog Hollow stand the state's first craft center (1975) and the Sheldon Museum, the oldest incorporated town museum in the nation. In an 1829 brick home, the museum displays an eclectic collection of artifacts of nineteenth-century New England life. It contains two handsomely appointed parlors, an old-fashioned country kitchen, a child's room complete with toys, dolls, and doll furniture, a country store, a tavern, extensive collections of pewter and Staffordshire, primitive portraits, and a library of old newspapers and other local historical records. The museum opens daily except Sundays and holidays from 10:00 a.m. to 5:00 p.m., June 1 to October 15. Admission is $1.00 for adults and $.50 for children. Frog Hollow Craft Center is open year-round except Sundays from 10:00 a.m. to 5:00 p.m. A panel of judges has selected all the works on display, and all are for sale.

Many pleasant restaurants and specialty shops line the streets of the village. There are also several places from which you can select food for lunch, and you can eat better by carrying a picnic with you than by shopping along the way.

You pass through the campus of Middlebury College just as you leave the village. Founded in 1800 and coeducational since 1883, Middlebury is a highly selective, rather traditional liberal arts college with about two thousand students. During the summer, programs leading to advanced degrees in foreign languages are run at the Middlebury Campus. On Bread Loaf Mountain in nearby Ripton, the College also offers a summer graduate program in English and American literature and a writers' conference, which Robert Frost helped found and taught for many years. The contemporary Christian A. Johnson Building, a hundred yards off the road on your right as you pass through the campus, displays paintings, sculptures, and graphics of students and professionals in its three-story open exhibition hall. The gallery is open to the public without charge daily from 1:00 p.m. to 5:00 p.m. The College provides free guided tours of its Middlebury campus from the Admissions Office in Emma Willard Hall (802-388-4929).

8.0   At the Stop Sign in Bridport, turn RIGHT to continue west on Route 125, which here runs concurrently with Route 22A North.

8.5   By Pratt's Store with BP gas pumps (on the left), turn LEFT to stay on Route 125 West.

12.0   By the farm with three silos (on the right), turn RIGHT onto Basin Harbor Road. You must look hard for this turn, for the street sign is on the left. In a mile and a half, after you cross Town Line Road, Basin Harbor Road becomes Jersey Street.

16.5   By Angier Farms (on the right), turn LEFT onto the unsigned road.

16.8   At the Stop Sign, turn LEFT onto Route 17 West. (There may not be a route marker at this intersection.)

17.8   At Franklin's Country Store with Amoco gas pumps (on the right) in West Addison, turn RIGHT onto Lake Street.

In just over a mile you have your first chance to swim in Lake Champlain. After passing a red house with a white fence on your left, turn left onto the Dead End road and ride a quarter-mile to the town beach. Though the beach is narrow and somewhat rocky, the water is clean and the swimming delightful. Lake Champlain covers 435 square miles, making it the sixth largest body of fresh water in the United States.

Over the next ten miles, as you glide through apple orchards and hayfields, the lake is often within sight. To your left across the water in New York State rise the Adirondack Mountains. And, provided the weather is clear, you can see the Green Mountains reaching across the eastern horizon, to your right. On the best of days you can see the five highest peaks in Vermont:

from south to north, Killington (el. 4,235′), Abraham (el. 4,052′), Ellen (el. 4,083′), Camel's Hump (el. 4,083′), and Mansfield (4,393′).

23.8   Turn RIGHT onto Pease Road.

24.6   At the T, turn LEFT onto Jersey Street.

Approach this turn cautiously. It comes suddenly when you are riding downhill, and sand often litters the road.

25.2   At the intersection in Panton, go STRAIGHT so you pass Daigneault's Store with Gulf gas pumps on your left.

Five miles from Panton, at the end of an unmarked road, lies Arnold Bay, which gained its name from a Revolutionary naval battle. In October, 1776, Benedict Arnold, who a year and a half earlier had accompanied Ethan Allen in the capture of Fort Ticonderoga, ingeniously outmaneuvered the larger British flotilla commanded by Admiral Guy Carleton. Carleton was

The cyclist still riding his bicycle doesn't know it yet, but he has just gotten a flat tire!

sailing his powerful fleet south to attack Ticonderoga and the fortifications on Mount Independence near Orwell, when Arnold stealthily attacked. Although Arnold lost much of his fleet, he nevertheless achieved his main objective of obstructing Carleton's progress and thereby delaying the British advance southward. Before they could assemble another offensive, the British were prevented from sailing because the lake had frozen. Rather than surrender even the battered ships he had used to block the British fleet, Arnold ran them aground off Panton and set them afire. The waterlogged hulls of these crafts are visible when the lake is low, and cannonballs and other relics of the encounter are still being uncovered.

25.7   At the fork, bear LEFT onto Sherman Road, which becomes Button Bay Road.

In a mile and a half you reach Button Bay State Park, on the lakeshore facing the Adirondack Mountains. The excellent swimming and picnic facilities make an enticing rest stop. Admission is $.75, and the park is open from the Friday before Memorial Day until mid-October from 10:00 a.m. until 9:00 p.m.

28.7   At the T, turn RIGHT onto Basin Harbor Road.

In about two miles you pass through an exceptionally fine marsh in the channel of Dead Creek. Here, on one thousand protected acres, diverse plantlife provides excellent habitats for migrating waterfowl, such as the Canada Goose, which passes through late every fall and early each spring.

33.0   At the Stop Sign, turn LEFT onto the unsigned road.

34.3   At the Stop Sign, turn LEFT onto West Main Street, which is Route 22A North, to enter Vergennes.

Vergennes is the last place to buy food until you reach Middlebury at the end of the tour. Several small markets offer an adequate selection for a picnic on the city's shaded green, which has its own drinking fountain. At the corner of the green, Painter's Tavern serves excellent lunches and dinners in a handsomely remodeled 1793 clapboard building.

Vergennes is built around a falls on Otter Creek, just eight navigable miles east of where that river empties into Lake Champlain. During the War of 1812 the British planned a land and naval offensive down Lake Champlain from Canada. In order to meet the British attack, thirty-year-old Captain Thomas Macdonough chose Vergennes as the place to winter (1813-14) and strengthen his fleet. In the shipyards of Vergennes new boats of Vermont timber were constructed in record time, and 177 tons of cannonballs were produced by the city's furnaces and forges. Thus fortified, Macdonough soundly defeated the British fleet of General Sir George Downie in a swift engagement that gave the United States undisputed control of the lake and saved Vermont from British occupation. This victory helped redeem Vermont's reputation for the widespread private smuggling of beef into Canada, where, according to General George Izard of the American army, it had been saving British forces from starvation.

34.8 Between Eris Portraits and the Gallery Restaurant (both on the right), turn RIGHT onto the unsigned road.

34.9 At the Stop Sign, go STRAIGHT across the intersection to continue south on the unsigned road from Vergennes.

41.0 At the Stop Sign, turn RIGHT onto Route 17 West. (There may be no route marker at this intersection.)

41.4 Turn LEFT onto Route 23 South.

In about three miles the tour's only difficult hill begins its mile-and-a-half climb into Weybridge Hill.

46.4 At Weybridge Hill, follow Route 23 through the intersection and then, immediately after passing the red brick Weybridge Congregational Church (on the left), turn LEFT onto Hamilton Road, which is unpaved. Do not turn onto either Cave Road or Sheep Farm Road, both of which are unpaved and intersect Hamilton Road. Hamilton Road can be soft, and it may be safer to walk in places.

47.8 At the T, turn RIGHT onto the paved, unsigned road.

In a half-mile the entrance to the Morgan Horse Farm, a National Historic Site, is on your left. Centered around a magnificent 1878 barn and run by the University of Vermont, the farm raises prize-winning Morgans and Aberdeen Angus cattle. The Morgan, Vermont's state animal, is the oldest breed of light horse developed in America, its lineage being traceable as far back as 1790. Though not a large horse, it possesses a wonderful variety of abilities and can be trained for plowing, cutting cattle, dressage, jumping, pleasure riding, show, police work, driving carts, and trotting. Morgans gain their name from Justin Morgan, a singing teacher and composer of some note, who brought his colt Figure here from Massachusetts nearly two hundred years ago. Colonel Joseph Battell of Middlebury established the farm, gave it to the United States in 1906, and compiled the original Morgan registry. His love for horses may have grown from his hatred of automobiles. While publisher of the Middlebury *Register*, Battell wrote a column entitled "Chamber of Horrors," where he dramatically described automobile accidents. The farm offers guided tours of its grounds and stables and a slide show about Morgans daily from 8:00 a.m. to 4:00 p.m., May 1 to November 1. The tour costs adults $1.75 and persons between thirteen and seventeen $.50. Children are not charged. There is no admission fee to the grounds and main barn.

49.3   At the tiny traffic island, bear LEFT and ride slowly and very carefully through the covered bridge.

Reaching 179 feet across the Otter Creek, the Pulpmill covered bridge is one of only two double-lane covered bridges in Vermont, the other being at the Shelburne Museum and not open to traffic.

49.9   One-tenth mile after you pass Barrera's Florist (on the right), turn LEFT and ride through the underpass.

50.0   Opposite Stan's Shop and Save Market (on the left), turn RIGHT onto the unsigned road.

50.5   At the Stop Sign, you are beside Middlebury's Congregational Church (1806), the magnificent product of Connecticut-born Lavius Fillmore, who also built the First Congregational Church in Bennington. The Middlebury Inn is a hundred yards away to your left.

Bicycle Shops

Bike & Ski Touring Center, 22 Main Street, Middlebury, VT   (802-388-6666)

Skihaus Mountain Sports, 56 Main Street, Middlebury, VT   (802-388-2823)

Vermont Bicycle Touring, Munger Street, New Haven, VT   (802-388-4011)

Northwestern Vermont

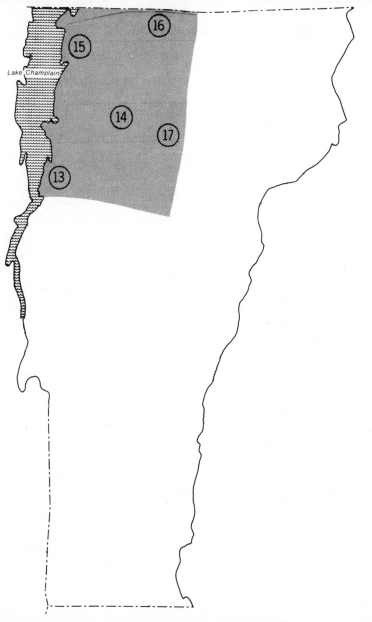

Lake Champlain

13

Shelburne-Hinesburg

Easy terrain; 18.5 miles

This tour offers an opportunity to combine a visit to one of the nation's greatest collections of American folk art with a short, delightfully pastoral ride in the Champlain Valley. Being both open and flat, the terrain not only affords panoramic views of the mountains but also makes the bicycling easy. Although nearly one-quarter of Vermont's 500,000 residents live within twenty-five miles of here, this route uses only quiet roads with little traffic. Shelburne, where the tour begins, has rightly acquired nationwide fame for its extraordinary museum. The village itself, shaded by sugar maples and old elms, boasts a variety of charming shops selling antiques, artworks, woodenware, crafts, foods, and country kitchenware.

0.0   From the blinker on US 7 in Shelburne, follow Mt. Philo Road south so you pass the Shelburne Country Store on your left.

If you have a half-day either before you begin cycling or afterwards, try to spend it at the Shelburne Museum. Nowhere in Vermont and few places in the United States display a finer or more varied collection of Americana. Founded in 1947 by Electra Havemeyer Webb, the Shelburne Museum consists of thirty-five buildings and the *S.S. Ticonderoga*, the last vertical beam passenger and freight sidewheeler remaining intact in this country. Spread over one hundred beautifully groomed and gardened acres on the west side of US 7, a quarter-mile south of the light at Mt. Philo Road, the museum is open daily from May 15 to October

15, between 9:00 a.m. and 5:00 p.m. Admission is $3.75 for adults, $2.00 for students of all ages, and free for children younger than seven. All Vermont teachers are admitted without charge. The museum realizes that even a cursory tour requires several hours, so it allows you to return the following day for $2.00 or, if you are a student, for free.

The museum reflects the eclectic taste of its founder, who began collecting American craft and folk art before its artistic merit was widely recognized. Many of the buildings are important historical artifacts themselves and were dismantled and moved

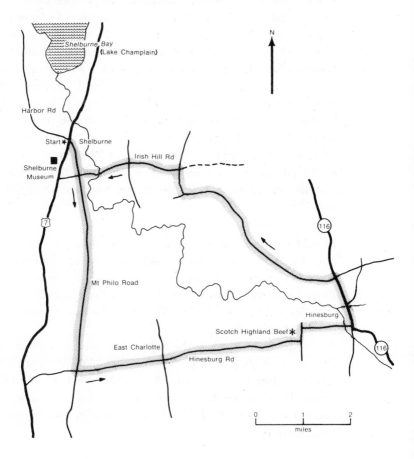

to Shelburne piece by piece. Four examples are: Prentis House (1733, Hadley, Massachusetts), a salt-box outfitted with seventeenth- and eighteenth-century furniture, delftware, and stumpwork embroidery; the Shelburne Railroad Station (1890), an example of Victorian architecture now filled with railroading memorabilia and beside which are parked a ten-wheel steam locomotive and an opulent private railroad car; a stagecoach inn (c. 1783, from nearby Charlotte), now housing sculptured folk art, including many cigar store Indians, trade signs, circus figures, and weathervanes; and Dorset House (c. 1840, East Dorset, Vermont) where Audubon prints, Joel Barber watercolors, and one thousand decoys are displayed. Among many other things, the museum contains a 525-foot-long scale model of a circus parade and two galleries of important paintings. The Webb Gallery features American primitive and academic works by Edward Hicks, Erastus Salisbury Field, Andrew Wyeth, Winslow Homer, and Albert Bierstadt among others. At the Electra Havemeyer Webb Building, in Georgian paneled rooms removed from the magnificent New York apartment of Mrs. Webb's in-laws, hang two paintings by Rembrandt and several by Monet as well as works of Manet, Whistler, Goya, Mary Cassatt, and Degas. The museum also has a cafeteria and picnic area.

Should you wish to buy food to carry while you are bicycling, stop by Harrington's, which sells its own smoked meats and Vermont cheeses, or the Shelburne Country Store. Both are located near the intersection of Mt. Philo Road and US 7.

0.7   At the Stop Sign, go STRAIGHT across the intersection and ride south on Mt. Philo Road.

From Mt. Philo Road, if the day is clear, you can make out the distinctive shape of Camel's Hump (el. 4,083'), Vermont's fourth tallest mountain, and also Mount Mansfield (el. 4,393'), the tallest. Both rise in the east to your left. To your right you can glimpse the Adirondack Mountains at one or two points if you look carefully.

4.6 At the Stop Sign, turn LEFT onto Hinesburg Road.

During the next six miles the road rolls over several small hills, providing roughly equal amounts of short climbs and descents.

6.4 At the blinker in East Charlotte, go STRAIGHT toward Hinesburg.

In about three and a half miles, as you turn a ninety-degree curve to the left, you may notice some peculiar cattle grazing in a small pasture by the road. These animals with reddish brown hair and long horns that can measure three feet in width are Scotch Highland Beef cattle.

10.8 At the Stop Sign in Hinesburg, turn LEFT onto Route 116 North toward Richmond.

At this turn you are facing Lantman Brothers IGA, the last place to buy food or drink until you return to Shelburne.

11.8 At the blinker, turn LEFT onto the unsigned road away from Champlain Valley Union High School.

Sometimes not everyone has to pedal

Between 2:30 p.m. and 4:00 p.m. on school days, traffic between here and Shelburne can be bothersome.

15.8   At the ninety-degree bend in the road, follow the main road to the RIGHT.

16.3   At the Stop Sign, turn LEFT onto Irish Hill Road.

17.3   At the crossroad, go STRAIGHT to continue on Irish Hill Road.

18.0   At the Stop Sign, turn RIGHT onto Mt. Philo Road.

18.5   You are now back in Shelburne where you began.

If you would like to go swimming, go straight at the blinker across US 7 onto Harbor Road. Then follow Harbor Road four miles to Shelburne Point on Lake Champlain, where you can swim off the rocks. Just after crossing US 7 you pass The Pottery, where Frank Mann makes and sells decorative and utilitarian stoneware, and the Shelburne Craft School Shop, which sells weavings, woodwork, pottery, stained glass, graphics, and jewelry made by its students and staff.

Bicycle Shops

Earl's Schwinn Cyclery, 142 Dorset Street, South Burlington, VT (802-864-9197 & 864-6190)

Pagocycle, 227 Main Street, Burlington, VT   (802-864-6878)

The Outfitters, Ethan Allen Shopping Center, Burlington, VT   (802-863-1257)

The Ski Rack Bike Shop, 81 Main Street, Burlington, VT   (802-658-3313)

Cambridge-Underhill Center

Moderate terrain; 24 miles

From the spacious, orderly old village of Cambridge, this tour etches a circle through farmlands at the base of Vermont's greatest mountain range. Few roads in the state make a more intimate connection with a mountain than aptly named Pleasant Valley Road makes with the massive profile of Mount Mansfield. It leads you along the western flank of the mountain at a distance just far enough away to appreciate its size and yet close enough to see in detail the rocks and vegetation on its slopes. Along the way you can also visit one of Vermont's most established potters and an experimental farm where scientists are studying the mysterious workings of sugar maples. The tour starts from Cambridge so you may ride on Route 15 as early in the day as possible. Route 15 draws more traffic than bicyclists normally need encounter in Vermont, but to ride it for ten miles in order to follow Pleasant Valley Road for fourteen makes it a fine bargain.

0.0   Leave Cambridge by riding west on Route 15.

        Cambridge was settled in 1783 during that extraordinary time when Vermont was an independent nation, 1777-91. The unusually wide thoroughfare in the center of the village was built so the local militia could hold their musters without interfering with traffic. Cambridge lies on a broad intervale along the Lamoille River, one of the few Vermont rivers canoeable in both spring and summer. Due to the ridge of mountains running like a spine through the center of the state, rivers in

Vermont generally flow down the eastern slope of the mountains into the Connecticut River or down the western slope into Lake Champlain. However the Lamoille, along with the Winooski and Missiquoi, are exceptions; rising in the east, they flow westward *through* the mountains to Lake Champlain. These rivers apparently anteceded the formation of the Green Mountains and when the latter rose were able to carve themselves valleys rapidly enough to maintain their courses. From Cambridge upstream to Johnson the Lamoille offers especially good cover for brown trout.

An interesting small botanical area of interest sits in a ravine behind the Cambridge cemetery. Called the Cambridge Pine

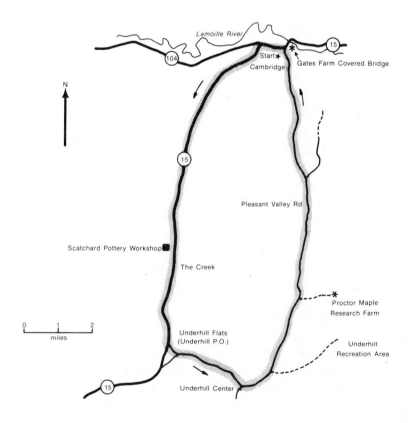

Woods after a stand of large white pine whose trunks measure as much as forty-eight inches in diameter, the Woods also contain hemlocks, sugar maples, red oaks, and herbs. At the eastern end of the village, near where Route 15 curves sharply over the Lamoille River, you can find the Gates Farm covered bridge. Built in 1897 and moved to its present site in 1951, its Burr Arch spans sixty feet.

0.7   At the intersection of Routes 15 and 104, turn LEFT to continue west on Route 15.

As soon as you make the turn, you start up a gentle to moderate hill a mile and a half long. Then, after a flat half-mile, the road tips downward into a gradual two-and-a-half-mile descent. As the descent fades away, the Scatchard Stoneware Workshop comes into view on your right. George Scatchard and his friends make lamps, tea pots, mugs, and dinnerware here; "If we don't have it, we'll make it for you." The workshop is open between 9:00 a.m. and 5:00 p.m., Monday through Friday. Past Scatchard's, Route 15 rolls uphill for a half-mile, downhill for three-quarters, and then uphill for another half-mile. From Scatchard's to Underhill Flats, keep a sharp look-out for wildlife for you are riding near a thousand-acre preserve called The Creek, where beavers have dammed a meandering stream, creating a series of ponds and extensive marshlands.

10.4   At the triangle (on the left) in Underhill Flats (Underhill P.O.), turn LEFT off Route 15 toward Underhill Center.

Settled in 1786, Underhill takes its name from its location under the wing of Mount Mansfield (el. 4,393'), Vermont's highest mountain. Within two hundred yards you come to Jacobs IGA Market on your right. You can find ample lunch supplies there to carry to one of the beautiful spots on Pleasant Valley Road for a picnic.

10.8   At the T, turn LEFT onto Pleasant Valley Road. (There is no street sign at this intersection.)

For the next two and three-quarter miles you follow the Browns River into the small, charming village of Underhill Center. You can buy more food there at the K & T Country Store on the left.

Taking a rest on the green in Underhill Flats

St. Thomas Catholic Church, which dominates the center of the village, contains several fine stained-glass windows. The Underhill Town Hall occupies the former Old White Church, built in 1850.

One mile north of the village you pass the entrance to the Underhill Recreation Area. Though this park is beautifully situated, it offers no swimming and is difficult to reach. The four-mile ride to get there goes up a precipitous grade on an unpaved road and is enjoyable only if you are seeking that sort of challenge.

Immediately beyond the entrance to the recreation area, you start a strenuous climb of a mile and a quarter. Then along a level half-mile you pass the driveway to the University of Vermont's Proctor Maple Research Farm. Throughout the year researchers from the Vermont Agricultural Experiment Station investigate ways to facilitate and improve the making of maple sugar products. During the sugaring season, which usually comes in March, sap is gathered and boiled into syrup on the farm. Visitors are welcome from 9:00 a.m. to 3:00 p.m., Monday through Friday, year-round. The mile-long, unpaved driveway into the farm runs mostly uphill.

You reach the height-of-land a mile beyond the entrance to the Maple Research Farm. There you can picnic in the shade of a sugar maple and look across rolling meadows to Mount Mansfield. From there back to Cambridge, seven and three-quarter miles away, you go downhill about half the time.

20.2 At the fork in Pleasant Valley, which consists only of this intersection, bear LEFT toward Cambridge.

24.0 At the Stop Sign by the Cambridge Lodge (1811), you are facing Route 15 back in Cambridge where the tour began.

Bicycle Shops

Demers Repair Inc., 81 South Main Street, Barre, VT   (802-476-7712)

Earl's Schwinn Cyclery, 142 Dorset Street, South Burlington, VT (802-864-9197 and 864-6190)

Jericho Sports, 7 LaFayette Drive, Jericho, VT   (802-899-3549)

Onion River Sports, 20 Langdon Street, Montpelier, VT   (802-229-9409)

Pagocycle, 227 Main Street, Burlington, VT   (802-864-6878)

The Outfitters, Essex Junction Shopping Center, Essex Junction, VT (802-879-7826)

The Ski Rack Bike Shop, 81 Main Street, Burlington, VT   (802-658-3313)

15

St. Albans-Swanton

Easy terrain; 25 miles

From St. Albans this tour follows a route without hills along the Missisquoi River and northern shore of Lake Champlain. Henry Ward Beecher thought St. Albans sat "in the midst of a greater variety of scenic beauty than any other [place] I can remember in America." That may still be largely true, but many changes have occurred in the hundred years since Beecher was writing. Trees have died or been removed to make way for construction, and houses have risen along the banks of the lake and river; so prepare yourself to feel occasionally frustrated by what humankind has done to this extraordinary region.

Nevertheless, the tour offers many beautiful views, a fine place to swim, and exceptional opportunities to see waterfowl and other migrating birds. Being short as well as level, it allows lots of time for exploration along the way. It also lends itself to cycling early and late in the season, for Lake Champlain tempers the climate, hastening spring and stalling winter. With no leaves on the trees the views are better, and with fewer vacationers about, the roads nearly yours alone. Moreover, if you do the tour in April, you can combine it with a visit to the Vermont Maple Sugar Festival in St. Albans. That is a joyous occasion, with sugar on snow, lumberjack contests, square dances, pancake breakfasts, a fiddling contest, and much more. (For scheduling information, write the Maple Festival Council, Box 255, St. Albans, VT 05478, or call 802-524-5800.)

0.0   From Taylor Park, the large green in the center of St. Albans, follow US 7 (North Main Street) North out of town.

St. Albans has witnessed some curious events in history because of its proximity to Canada. Before the railroad reached St. Albans, potash was the city's only saleable product, and Montreal its only market. But in 1807 the passage of Thomas Jefferson's Embargo Act forbade trade with all foreign nations, and the good folk of St. Albans became deeply involved in smuggling. One St. Albans merchant hired a craft, named *Black Snake*, to run potash into Canada. His business thrived for several months until the border patrol discovered *Black Snake* and chased it down Lake Champlain. At Burlington a bloody battle ensued with the smugglers killing three federal officers and wounding several others before losing their craft. Opposition to the Embargo Act ran so deeply in Vermont, as it did throughout New England, that only one of the smugglers was executed. The others were imprisoned and subsequently pardoned.

With the completion of the railroad in 1850, prosperity came to St. Albans. Ironically that prosperity also indirectly caused the most memorable day in St. Albans's history. At three o'clock in the afternoon of October 19, 1864, twenty-two rebel soldiers seeking funds for the Confederacy converged on St. Albans. Simultaneously they entered all the banks, unburdened them of over $200,000, killed one man, and wounded several others. They then hustled their booty across the border to Canada, burning the Sheldon covered bridge behind them. Thus did St. Albans become the site of the Civil War's northernmost engagement, if that it can be called. The Franklin-Lamoille Bank at 8 North Main Street has photomurals of the raid and helped publish a pamphlet about it in 1971.

Other mementos of the raid, including some of the stolen currency and a broadside entitled "Orleans County Awake, Rebels in Vermont!", are exhibited at the Franklin County Museum, which faces the eastern end of Taylor Park. The museum's large and diverse collection also contains two interesting medical exhibits. One consists of the memorabilia of William Beaumont, a surgeon who studied in St. Albans from 1810 to 1812 and contributed greatly to medical research by reporting on the digestive system of a patient who had a permanent hole in his stomach from a gunshot wound. The other exhibit contains the furnishings from Dr. George Russell's Arlington, Vermont, office, made famous by Norman Rockwell in his painting, "The Family Doctor," which appeared on a 1947 cover of *The Saturday Evening Post*.

On your way out of St. Albans, you can get all sorts of good things to eat, including excellent sandwiches, at the attractive natural foods store called Whole Grain. Located at 77 North Main Street, the store is open from 9:30 a.m. to 5:30 p.m., Monday through Saturday. You pass two especially fine old houses: the Stranahan House (c. 1850) at 149 North Main and the city's oldest building, the Hoyt House, formerly a tavern built in 1793, at 255 North Main Street. Other buildings worth seeing are the Houghton House, built in 1801 and now a national historic site and realtor's office, at 86 South Main Street, and the Congregational Church and the Franklin County Court House, both of which face Taylor Park near the museum. Finally, you might stop by the Vermont Information Center at 128 North Main Street to inquire whether any special events are taking place while you are in the area.

Bicycling on US 7 requires your complete attention. Not only is the traffic usually heavy, but vehicles may be backing out of diagonal parking spaces, stopping suddenly, turning onto the road, and turning off it without signaling properly.

2.1 Bear RIGHT off US 7 onto the road toward Highgate Center and Interstate 89.

Just before reaching the next turn, you can get a good look off to your right at Jay Peak (el. 3,861') and the other mountains in that range, if the weather is clear.

6.4 At the crossroad, turn LEFT onto the unsigned road.

7.5 At the Stop Sign, turn RIGHT onto US 7 North.

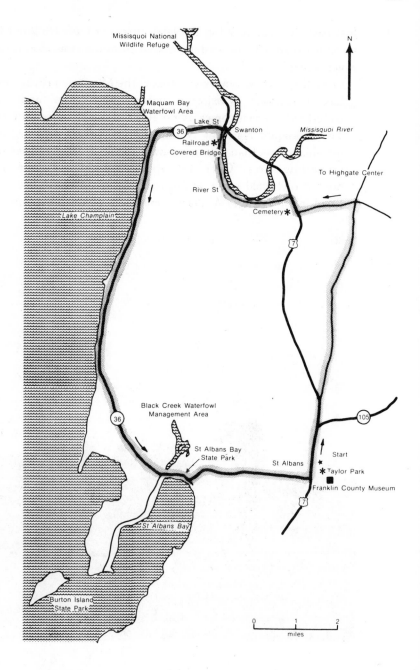

7.8   Just past the cemetery (on the left), turn LEFT off US 7 onto the unsigned road. (At its western end in Swanton, this road is called River Street.)

Over the next two miles you follow the Missisquoi River toward Lake Champlain. Missisquoi means "much grass" and "many waterfowl," which comes as no surprise once you see the river. The Missisquoi National Wildlife Refuge covers 4,792 acres of marshland less than five miles away so you are likely to see some interesting birds. Over 180 species—including osprey, great horned owl, bald eagle, and great blue heron—have been identified in the refuge. A quarter-mile before your next turn, you

Until recently there were more cows than people in Vermont

pass the Swanton Railroad covered bridge. Built in 1898, the three spans of this bridge measure 369 feet, making it the longest railroad covered bridge still standing in Vermont.

10.8   On the outskirts of Swanton, turn LEFT onto Lake Street, which is Route 36 East. (You can easily miss this turn, and, if you do, you immediately pass a Hire's Root Beer sign and an antique shop on the right and then reach a Stop Sign.)

The antique shop merits a look. If the door is locked, you can call the owner Gordon Winters at 802-868-3322 or find him at the Swanton Lumber Company, one block straight ahead from the Stop Sign. Winters sells an interesting assortment of furniture, clocks, and other collectibles; in 1977 I bought a nineteenth-century wooden-wheel, safety bicycle from him.

Like St. Albans, Swanton is no stranger to smuggling. The bootleggers of the Roaring Twenties who drove Canadian whiskey into Vermont here were the spiritual descendents of Vermont farmers who drove cattle into Canada to sell them to the starving British soldiers during the War of 1812.

Each year near the end of July, Swanton produces a Summer Festival that includes art and craft exhibits, band concerts, barbershop quartet singing, a lumberjack roundup, a chicken barbecue, a parade, and a fairway with rides and concessions. For details and a schedule, contact the Swanton Chamber of Commerce, Box 182, Swanton, VT 05488 (802-868-7200).

A mile and three-quarters after turning onto Route 36, you pass the Maquam Bay Waterfowl Area, reach Lake Champlain, and begin a six-mile ride along its shoreline. The sixth largest body of fresh water in the United States, Lake Champlain covers 435 square miles and stretches 118 miles down Vermont's western border. In the winter the lake freezes to a depth of nearly two feet and supports a multitude of fishing shanties. Although private homes, cottages, and trees occasionally obstruct your view, you can often see across the lake to the Adirondack Mountains. A mile and a quarter after the road pulls away from the lakeshore, Camel's Hump (el. 4,083'), Vermont's fourth highest peak, looms into view far in the southeast. Once you know its name, you can always identify it.

21.0 The road to Burton Island State Park branches off Route 36 to the right.

Burton Island offers the best swimming and picnicking on the tour. To reach the park, turn right here and ride three and a half miles along the shoreline of St. Albans Bay to Lake Champlain. From there you must take a boat, for which the charge is $2 per boatload, and leave your bicycle on the mainland. You can arrange to have a boat meet you by calling 802-524-6353, but you may find a boat there when you arrive anyway. The 253-acre island remains undeveloped except the sites set aside for camping, swimming, and picnicking. Admission is $.75.

21.7 The entrance to St. Albans Bay State Park is on your right.

This park also offers swimming and provides a snack bar as well. Unfortunately the waters of St. Albans Bay are slightly polluted and consequently nuture weeds and algae, which make the swimming less pleasant than at Burton Island. Admission to this state park is also $.75.

21.9 At Booth's Market (with Arco gas pumps on the left), turn LEFT to follow Route 36 East.

In three miles, just as you reenter St. Albans, you pass some of the grand railroad architecture for which the city is rightly known. Most of the buildings seem neglected, but the thought and aesthetic considerations which went into their design are clearly evident.

25.0 At the traffic light, you are facing Taylor Park where the tour began.

Bicycle Shops

Bushey's Sporting Goods Store, 15 Kingman Street, St. Albans, VT   (802-524-3577)

Earl's Schwinn Cyclery, 142 Dorset Street, South Burlington, VT (802-864-9197 & 864-6190)

Pagocycle, 227 Main Street, Burlington, VT   (802-864-6878)

The Outfitters, Essex Junction Shopping Center, Essex Junction, VT (802-879-7826)

The Ski Rack Bike Shop, 81 Main Street, Burlington, VT   (802-658-3313)

16

Enosburg Falls-Richford

Moderate-to-difficult terrain; 33.5 miles

Beginning in the town of Enosburg Falls, this tour offers unsurpassed bicycling along the Vermont-Quebec border. Few places in the United States have such extraordinary beauty and roads as free of traffic as northwestern Vermont. The tour winds its way through rolling farmlands fringed by thousands of sugar maples and bounded by the mountains. Falling at the northern end of the Green Mountain chain, the route is relatively hilly, though it never crosses a mountain pass, and so warrants a moderate-to-difficult rating. But the undulations of the terrain provide cyclists with several superb downhill runs and many sweeping views of the mountains. Following the Missisquoi and Trout rivers along its final and easiest third, the tour also passes three old covered bridges.

0.0 From the Enosburg Falls green follow Route 108 North toward West Berkshire.

Before leaving town, you might want to get some food to carry along, since there are no groceries or restaurants until Richford, fourteen miles away.

One of a few towns that the Republic of Vermont chartered during its fourteen years as an independent nation (1777-91), Enosburg Falls is now best known for maple syrup and the springtime Vermont Dairy Festival. Held just outside the village on the first Saturday of June, the Festival features a parade, livestock shows, horse pulling contests, barbecues, and lots of country

119

fiddling and square dancing. Though it draws considerable traffic to the area, only Route 105 is usually affected. It would be fun to combine an early springtime ride with a visit to the Dairy Festival.

In the early nineteenth century an Enosburg settler named Isaac Farrar developed wooden spouts for tapping sugar maple trees. Though the effectiveness of the spouts quickly led to their widespread use, Farrar's neighbors nevertheless accused him of "scientific farming," which then was not the vogue that it is now. Later in the nineteenth century Enosburg Falls acquired a substantial reputation as the home of panaceas and patent medicines, "guaranteed" to cure nearly every ill of man or beast. At least four local entrepreneurs amassed fortunes with their cures, and some people say that descendants of the original manufacturers still pursue the business.

Route 108 goes gently uphill much of the way to West Berkshire. About two and a half miles north of Enosburg Falls, stop to take a look at the view behind you. To the east stands Jay Peak (el.

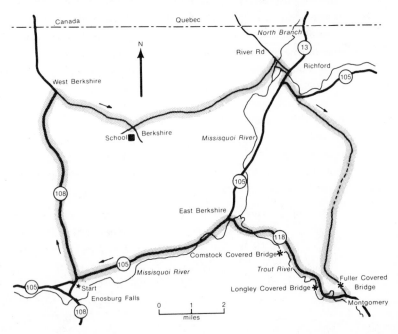

3,861'), readily identifiable by its cone-shaped top on which a ski lift now perches. Mount Mansfield, at 4,393' the state's tallest summit, rises directly behind you in the south.

6.0 At the Stop Sign in West Berkshire, turn RIGHT off Route 108 onto the unnumbered road toward Berkshire. (Just after making this turn, you pass an Arco station on your left.)

Should you want to go into Canada, you can get there easily by continuing north two miles further on Route 108. You should carry at least a driver's license as identification, if you actually cross the border and so have to reenter the United States. About twelve miles northwest of West Berkshire at Eccles Hill in Quebec, the Fenians, a secret Irish brotherhood organized in the 1850s to gain independence for Ireland, marshalled an attack on Canada in 1870. Nearly a thousand Fenians came to Vermont by train from Boston. They fought one small battle—the only violent encounter of their unsuccessful attempt to acquire land for a New Ireland—and then fled back across the border, where the U.S. Marshal promptly arrested their leaders.

8.6 At the crossroad by the Berkshire Elementary School (on the right), turn LEFT onto the unsigned road.

For about a mile you must climb a moderate grade, but then the road turns downward into a wonderful four-mile descent facing one of the most panoramic views in Vermont. Directly before you stands the Jay Peak range; to your left in Canada the hump of Pinnacle Mountain rises above the hills; and on the clearest of days Mount Mansfield is visible far to the south, over your right shoulder.

13.7 At the T, turn RIGHT onto River Road. (There may not be a street sign at this intersection, but you immediately cross a bridge, and in a quarter-mile you pass an Arco station on your right.)

14.2 At the blinker in Richford, turn RIGHT, cross the bridge over the Missiquoi River, and follow the signs onto Route 105 East.

Richford stands in the midst of great natural beauty, but the village bears the scars of misfortune and adversity. More than once ravaged by fire and flooding, Richford has recently also suffered economic hardship as the hardwood lumber businesses that once supported much of the town have fallen on hard times.

Downhill toward Montgomery

But in March and April the area comes alive with sugarmaking, for Richford stands near the center of Franklin County, the largest syrup-producing area in Vermont.

There are several small supermarkets and a luncheonette in Richford.

15.2   Turn RIGHT off Route 105 onto the unsigned road. (You immediately pass beneath a railroad trestle and go up a steep hill.)

The hill rises steeply for about three-quarters of a mile and then continues gradually for two miles more to the end of the pavement. The road then becomes unpaved for one and a half miles and should be ridden very cautiously on its downhill portions. Just before the road ends at the outskirts of Montgomery it passes through the Fuller or Blackfalls covered bridge, built over Black Falls Creek in 1890 by Sheldon and Savannah Jewett.

22.5   At the Stop Sign in Montgomery, turn RIGHT onto Route 118 North.

On your right before you leave the village is the Montgomery Village Store, the last place you can buy food until you reach Enosburg Falls.

Off the southwestern side of Route 118—to the left as you ride toward East Berkshire—are two more covered bridges, also built by the Jewetts. Both stretch eighty feet across the Trout River and shade good swimming and fishing holes. You reach the first, known as Longley or Harnois bridge, a mile and a half from Montgomery; it went into use in 1863. The second, the Comstock bridge, was erected twenty years later and is visible two miles after the first.

27.5   At the Stop Sign in East Berkshire, turn LEFT onto Route 105 West.

Route 105 has considerably more traffic than any other road on this tour and crosses railroad tracks several times.

33.5   You are back in Enosburg Falls with the green on your left.

Bicycle Shops

Bushey's Sporting Goods Store, 15 Kingman Street, St. Albans, VT   (802-524-3577)

J & R Sports, Jay, VT   (802-988-2857)

17

Stowe-Morrisville

Easy-to-moderate terrain; 21 miles

Following delightfully untrafficked roads north of Stowe, this tour
affords magnificent views of Mount Mansfield and the peaks that
surround it. By heading directly into the countryside, you neatly
avoid Stowe's tourist accommodations and cycle through an arcadia
of small farms and fishing ponds. Nevertheless, because the tour
is short, you also have time to visit the "Ski Capital of the East."
In fact Stowe is also a warm weather sports center, offering tennis,
bicycle racing, horseback riding, rock climbing, hiking, swimming,

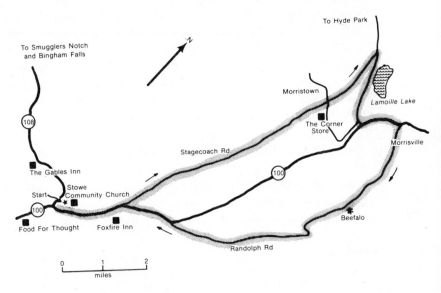

fishing, and golfing on the highest course in the state. There is a competitive edge to the place; year-round most residents of Stowe seem to be working out, sharpening a technique, or mastering some new sport. But despite all this activity and attractions such as the Green Mountain Guild summer theater, Stowe, more than any other skiing center in the state, retains its integrity as a Vermont village: unhurried, independent, and friendly. The goings-on in the area change constantly and are too numerous to list, but you can get information from the Stowe Area Association on Main Street. The tour begins at the Stowe Community Church (1863), whose graceful, slim spire soars high above the adjacent buildings.

0.0   From the Stowe Community Church follow Route 100 (Main Street) North.

Since there is little opportunity to buy food along the route, you should probably get something before leaving town. Food for Thought, on the east side of Route 100 about one mile south of the church, purveys an extensive selection of natural foods, which you can buy by weight. It also makes delicious, mostly vegetarian, sandwiches on its own whole-grain breads. Delicatessen fare is available in town at Val's Market opposite the church. Or you can treat yourself to a delicious breakfast at The Gables Inn, a mile and a half out of town on Route 108. Innkeepers Sol and Lynn Baumrind serve homemade specialties from 8 a.m. till noon at tables on their lawn facing Mount Mansfield.

1.6   At the Foxfire Inn (on the right), bear LEFT off Route 100 onto Stagecoach Road. (There may not be a street sign there.)

After a mile and a half of relatively level terrain, Stagecoach Road curves uphill for one and two-tenths miles, then levels off for about three-quarters of a mile, and turns uphill again for a half-mile. Once you reach the top, all the difficult climbing of the tour is behind you, and you immediately begin to reap dividends. From the crest the road runs downhill for over a mile to Morristown.

Mount Mansfield, as seen from the north

Along Stagecoach Road you get your first long views of Mount Mansfield, at 4,393′ Vermont's highest peak, and its surrounding mountains—Dewey (el. 3,360′), Spruce Peak (el. 3,320′), Madonna (el. 3,640′), and White Face (el. 3,715′).

7.5 At the Stop Sign beside The Corner Store in Morristown, go STRAIGHT to continue north on Stagecoach Road.

The road shoots downhill again for over a mile. The last half of the hill is steep, occasionally sandy, and ends abruptly at an intersection, so take it slowly and carefully.

8.8   At the T, turn RIGHT onto the unsigned road.

Within a half-mile you are cycling along Lamoille Lake on your left.

10.2   At the Yield Sign, turn LEFT onto the unsigned road toward Stowe.

10.3   At the Stop Sign, turn LEFT onto Route 100 North.

11.0   At the traffic island on the edge of Morrisville, turn RIGHT onto Randolph Road.

In about three miles you reach a pasture on the left where you may see a few wooly red-haired cattle. These rather wild-looking animals are Beefalo, a cross between buffalo and domestic beef cattle.

Soon on your right a sweeping view of the Mount Mansfield

range comes into sight. If you use your imagination, you may be able to discern a resemblance between Mansfield and the profile of a human face with forehead, nose, lips, chin, and Adam's apple. After completing your bicycle tour, consider going to the top of Mansfield. You can get there by hiking, driving the toll road, or taking the Mount Mansfield Gondola ($3.50 round trip), which runs on Memorial Day weekend and from mid-June to September. The views from the summit are among the most spectacular in Vermont.

18.6   At the Stop Sign, bear LEFT onto Route 100 South.

21.0   You are back in Stowe by the Community Church.

If the weather is hot and you are feeling like a swim, nothing can rival Bingham Falls, where the West Branch of Little River tumbles through a shaded glen below Smugglers Notch into deep pools of sparkling, cold water. The falls are located about two hundred yards off the east side of Route 108, four and a half miles north of its intersection with Route 100. There is a parking area on the west side of the road across from the path that leads through the woods to the waterfalls.

After your swim, consider continuing north on Route 108 three and a half miles to Smugglers Notch. The Notch, a pass between Mount Mansfield and Sterling Mountain, reaches an elevation of 2,162 feet. It earned its name during the War of 1812 when smugglers took cattle and other commodities through it to Canada in violation of Thomas Jefferson's Embargo Acts. The temperature in the Notch is always markedly lower than elsewhere in the vicinity and sustains rare Ice Age flora not found even at higher elevations. Thousand-foot cliffs rise on either side of the road, and you can frequently see rock climbers clinging to the outcroppings. In the annual June Stowe Bicycle Race cyclists must climb through the Notch twice on the eighty-six mile course, over which they average nearly twenty-five miles an hour!

Bicycle Shops

Demers Repair, Inc., 81 South Main Street, Barre, VT   (802-476-7712)

Onion River Sports, 20 Langdon Street, Montpelier, VT   (802-229-9409)

Shaw's General Store, Main Street, Stowe, VT   (802-253-4040)

Northeastern Vermont

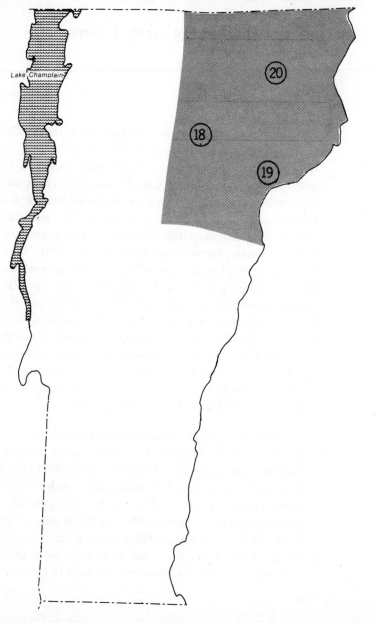

Lake Champlain

18

Wolcott-Craftsbury Common

Difficult terrain; 38 miles

Starting in Wolcott, this tour explores an extraordinary pocket of Vermont's Northeast Kingdom. Named by former U.S. Senator George Aiken, the Northeast Kingdom is roughly a square, forty miles on a side, bordering Canada and New Hampshire. Long an economic backwater, this region of glacial lakes and conifer forests possesses a sort of pastoral magic. The path taken by this tour is no exception, although Craftsbury Common and Greensboro no longer suffer from economic hardship. In that respect the tour highlights an especially privileged part of the Kingdom. But the magic persists: in Caspian Lake, in the nearly deserted road winding its way through the Craftsburys, and in North Wolcott, where lives of hardship in the midst of beauty are still the rule. Spend a full day making the tour, if you can, for few places offer better opportunities to meet such a diversity of friendly people than do Wolcott, Hardwick, Greensboro, and Craftsbury Common. The difficult portion of the tour comes in its first half, and the final third is as easy as it is beautiful.

0.0 Leave Wolcott on Route 15 East toward Hardwick.

Settled in 1789, Wolcott was named after General Oliver W. Wolcott, one of the signers of the Declaration of Independence. You start from this rather drab town in order to complete most of the cycling on Route 15 at the beginning of the tour. As the main thoroughfare across the northern quarter of Vermont, Route 15 draws a substantial amount of traffic, including many trucks. Cycling on this road is usually most pleasant in the morning. Over the six miles from Wolcott to Hardwick you climb very slightly uphill along the Lamoille River, which rises north of Greensboro and flows west into Lake Champlain.

Two miles east of Wolcott on your right, the Fisher covered bridge extends 103 feet over the Lamoille River. Built in 1908 by the St. Johnsbury and Lamoille Railroad Company, it is the last railroad covered bridge in use in Vermont and one of only a few left in the country. A cupola, which runs its full length to provide a vent for the smoke, distinguishes this covered bridge from others. Scheduled for replacement in 1968, the bridge was saved by private donations and state funds, which paid for the installation of supportive steel beams beneath its floor.

5.8 At the T in front of the Hardwick Department Store, turn LEFT to continue on Route 15 East. The next two turns come within a quarter-mile.

If you feel like swimming, instead of turning left at this T, turn right onto Route 14 South, ride a half-mile, and then turn left toward Mackville. Follow that road three-quarters of a mile to a picnic and swimming area on the right by Mackville Pond.

Hardwick was a simple agricultural town until 1868, when Henry R. Mack discovered granite there. Then the area went through a dramatic transformation, becoming one of the granite centers of the nation. Like a booming mining town, it rode the crest of prosperity into a period of frenetic, haphazard growth which has left a rather unattractive architectural legacy. If you are interested in old glass, stop at the Hardwick Pharmacy before you leave town. On display there is a superb collection of apothecary jars more than a century old.

Hardwick has recently gained statewide attention as the home of the Craftsbury Chamber Players. This group of skilled professionals, who teach and perform in metropolitan areas most of the year, gives concerts each Thursday during July and August at 8:30 p.m. They choose to play in the Hardwick Town House because of its exceptional acoustics. In September Hardwick hosts a major banjo contest; you can get the dates from the Hardwick Town Clerk on Church Street (802-472-5971).

You can buy food at several stores in Hardwick or later in Greensboro and Craftsbury.

5.9 Immediately past a Gulf station (on the left), turn LEFT off Route 15 onto the unsigned road, which immediately crosses a green iron bridge over the Lamoille River.

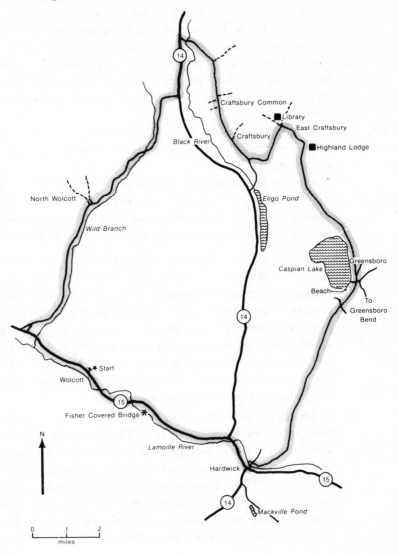

6.0   At the crossroad by the large gray stone Memorial Building (on the right), turn RIGHT onto another unsigned road.

The Memorial Building, constructed of local granite, contains a room made of Proctor, Vermont, marble and houses a valuable collection of old coins and paper currency.

This section of the tour is its most strenuous. For the first mile and a half the road rises steadily and steeply. Then after descending for a mile, it rolls over smaller hills for three miles, gaining elevation till it reaches Greensboro at an elevation of 1,463', 800 feet above Hardwick.

11.8   At the crossroad, go STRAIGHT toward Greensboro.

In three-quarters of a mile you can see on your left a small sign for a public beach indicating the quarter-mile-long road to Caspian Lake. Surrounded by low hills and wooded shores, Caspian ranks as one of Vermont's most beautiful and undisturbed large lakes. Its crystalline waters are fed by springs and offer splendid swimming from a sandy shore at the edge of a parklike lawn maintained by the town of Greensboro.

12.6   In the village of Greensboro, bear LEFT toward East Craftsbury—and away from Greensboro Bend.

You can get food for a picnic at Willey's Store in town, just a stone's throw from the entrance to the lake. Greensboro has become a rather expensive summer retreat favored especially by writers and professors.

12.8   At the curve, keep LEFT to follow the main road.

Over the next three miles, the road rolls up and down several short hills and then goes downhill for four miles into East Craftsbury. At the crest of the hill by the Highland Lodge it is worth stopping to look at the view of Caspian Lake.

As you swing through a sharp left curve in East Craftsbury, you pass the John Woodruff Simpson Memorial Library on the right. Formerly a community store, this pleasing little building has been imaginatively transformed. Books and magazines now line the shelves where groceries and dry goods were once stacked, and the spacious interior makes a comfortable reading room.

Pedaling by the Congregational Church in Craftsbury Common

Just beyond the library, the road bends into an exhilarating two-mile descent into the Black River Valley.

20.1 At the Stop Sign, turn RIGHT onto the unsigned road that goes through Craftsbury to Craftsbury Common.

You reach Craftsbury in one mile. If you are not carrying food or have not already eaten, you should stop at one of the two stores there, because they are the last ones on the route. Since Craftsbury Common is much more beautiful and interesting than Craftsbury, it is worth waiting to picnic there.

Though barely over a mile long, the ride up to the broad plateau where Craftsbury Common sits is demanding. But at the top you suddenly find yourself in an almost surreal collection of trim houses, uniformly gleaming with white clapboards and green shutters, and commanding views across verdant valleys to mountains in the east and west. Entirely free of commercial establishments—save two craft shops and Penny and Michael Schmitt's exquisitely tasteful Inn on the Common—this airy village surrounding a broad green must be one of the most memorable in New England. Its spotless neatness accentuates the simplicity of line and color in its architecture. Giant elms and sugar maples shade lawns set behind white picket fences. And elegantly presiding over the village is the towering spire of the splendid Congregational Church (1820).

Twice a year—on Saturdays in late July and mid-September— the Common's spell of silent dignity is broken by the sounds of country music and clapping hands. On these two weekends the village hosts old-time fiddling and banjo contests. Drawing performers from throughout New England, these occasions also attract as many as 10,000 spectators. The contests are wonderful fun, if you have the taste and energy for a day of music, revelry, and dancing, but they wreak havoc with local traffic patterns and should consequently be avoided unless you are planning your bicycle tour as a way to attend. Even then, since the music lasts well into the night, you should not plan to return to Wolcott afterwards. Information about the Craftsbury contests and others can be obtained by writing to the Northeast Fiddlers Association, c/o Wayne Perry, R.D. 1, Stowe, VT 05672.

22.3   From Craftsbury Common, continue to follow the main road STRAIGHT through town, keeping the common on your left.

From the Common you glide speedily downhill nearly three miles back into the Black River valley.

25.0   At the Stop Sign, turn LEFT onto Route 14 South.

27.0   Turn RIGHT off Route 14 onto the unsigned road toward North Wolcott.

You ride gently uphill for a mile and then follow the Wild Branch River till it empties into the Lamoille beside Route 15.

36.0   Bear RIGHT at the fork, go a hundred yards to the Stop Sign, and there turn LEFT onto Route 15 East.

38.0   You reach Wolcott where this tour began.

Bicycle Shops

Lyndon Cycle Shop, 72 Broad Street, Lyndon, VT   (802-626-5334)

Onion River Sports, 20 Langdon Street, Montpelier, VT   (802-229-9409)

Park Pedals, Town Highway II, Cabot, VT   (802-563-2252)

Shaw's General Store, Main Street, Stowe, VT   (802-253-4040)

McIndoe Falls-St. Johnsbury

Moderate-to-difficult terrain; 57 or 41 miles

From the tiny settlement of McIndoe Falls, this tour reaches northward along the Connecticut River uplands, dubbed the Northeast Kingdom by former U.S. Senator George Aiken. The first fifteen miles of bicycling bring challenge along with beauty as you leave the river valley and ride westward into the hills of Caledonia County. The terrain in this section of the route is sometimes arduous, but the charm of the Kingdom's tiny towns and the views of its undulating hills make the effort dramatically worthwhile. At its midpoint the tour enters St. Johnsbury and necessitates a little cycling on roads that are neither pretty nor quiet. But that city offers surprising attractions as well: a fine museum of natural history, a remarkable art gallery, and a comprehensive exhibit of the process of making maple syrup. The tour abandons Vermont for New Hampshire in the final twelve miles. There you follow the Connecticut River through pleasing farmlands from which you get rare, long views across the river to the Vermont villages of Lower Waterford and Barnet.

0.0   From McIndoe Falls follow US 5 North toward St. Johnsbury.
  The McIndoe Falls Inne, at the center of the few buildings that constitute the village, serves delicious organically raised food and contains a small health food store.

2.8   After crossing Stephens River at Barnet, turn LEFT toward West Barnet, Harveys Lake, and Peacham. Ride twenty yards to the fork and bear LEFT. In a hundred yards, you pass Dunbar Plumbing Company on your right.

During the first week of October, Barnet joins Peacham and other towns in the area to sponsor the Northeast Kingdom Annual Fall Foliage Festival. The celebration lasts a week and a different event is scheduled in each town daily.

3.2 At the Stop Sign just beyond Barnet village, turn RIGHT toward Peacham.

A mile and a half out of Barnet you pass a Buddhist meditation center, which sits on 430 acres to your right. Visitors are welcome.

5.9 After passing (on the left) a small springhouse with a red roof—it looks like the cupola on a barn—go STRAIGHT.

The next four and a half miles are the most difficult of the tour. Rolling hill follows rolling hill as you climb out of the Connecticut River valley into the uplands of Peacham. From an elevation of 452′ at Barnet you climb through West Barnet to 1,000′ at South Peacham and then, in barely over a mile, 900′ more to Peacham (el. 1,908′).

7.7 At the Lakeview Grange in West Barnet, bear LEFT so you pass a church on your left and then the West Barnet General Store on your right.

8.1 Just beyond the Exxon pumps in West Barnet, turn RIGHT toward Peacham.

9.4 At the T in front of the South Peacham Store, turn RIGHT toward Peacham and Danville.

10.5 In Peacham continue STRAIGHT past the Peacham General Store (on the left).

Peacham contains several eighteenth-century buildings and a friendly general store. The Peacham Historical Society merits a visit by anyone intrigued with local history. Its hours are irregular, but you can get a key from the Town Clerk or by calling Mrs. Erlene Moore at 802-592-3563.

From Peacham to Danville the cycling is easier. Although the terrain continues to roll, you lose almost 600′ in elevation over the next six miles.

17.2   At the blinker in Danville, go STRAIGHT across US 2 onto the
unsigned road to North Danville.

Danville sits on a plateau, commanding long views of New
Hampshire's White Mountains. Thaddeus Stevens was born
here in 1792. A vigorous and outspoken opponent of slavery, he
also fought Lincoln's plan for reconstructing the south after
the Civil War because he considered it too lenient. Leader of the

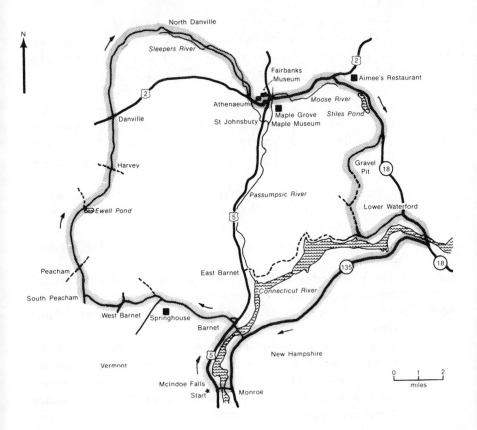

Congressional Radical Republicans, Stevens broke with Andrew Johnson when the latter vetoed a bill to protect the newly freed blacks from vengeful codes being legislated against them by many southern states. Stevens went on to lead the successful battle for the Fourteenth Amendment and to conduct the House impeachment proceedings against Johnson.

In some circles Danville is best known as the dowsing headquarters of the nation. Dowsers locate water and other underground objects by moving a forked stick over the ground until the stick bends downward to indicate a find. For over eighty years members of the American Society of Dowsers have been convening here for a weekend in September to swap stories and trade secrets. On the Sunday morning of that weekend a crowd of dowsers and onlookers always gathers on the green as everyone who wants to try dowsing is given a chance. A good dowser can unsettle the crustiest skeptic. You can obtain further information about dowsing and the Society by writing to the Secretary, American Society of Dowsers, Inc., Danville, VT 05828.

You can buy food, including fresh fruits and vegetables, at the Danville General Store across from the green. The next ten miles offer many pleasant places to picnic. After climbing for a mile, you glide downhill nearly nine miles to St. Johnsbury, which lies at an elevation of 655', more than 700' lower than Danville.

28.0 At the blinker in St. Johnsbury, turn LEFT onto US 2 East and follow it through town. (If you want to reduce the tour to forty-one miles, take US 5 South from St. Johnsbury thirteen miles to McIndoe Falls. US 5 follows the Passumpsic River and makes easy riding. Much of the traffic that formerly used US 5 now takes Interstate 91.)

Situated at the confluence of the Passumpsic, Moose, and Sleepers rivers, St. Johnsbury with a population of 8,400 is the largest town in the Northeast Kingdom. Much of its history and architecture derives from the imagination and generosity of Thaddeus Fairbanks (1796-1886), inventor of the lever scale and founder of the Fairbanks-Morse Scale Works. Many of the

Cycling a quiet road in the Northeast Kingdom

grand homes and public buildings along Main Street (US 2) were built between 1830 and 1870, when the company's prosperity led to the tripling of the city's population.

Three things in St. Johnsbury are particularly interesting. The Fairbanks Museum of Natural Science at 83 Main Street is the city's most elegant architectural work. Lambert Packard designed it in the Richardsonian style with a facade of red sandstone and a finely crafted interior featuring an arched oak ceiling and spiral staircases. The museum contains a comprehensive display of Vermont flora, one of the world's largest collections of hummingbirds, and an eclectic assortment of other objects. Adults and children alike can spend hours marveling at mounted animals from throughout the world, a mummy case, a suit of armor, old china, pewter, fossils, minerals, and much more. In the basement physical phenomena are cleverly presented by push-button displays that almost ask to be manipulated. Outside, live owls, hawks, reptiles, and small animals are exhibited in natural habitats. During the summer the museum also sponsors nature walks to see birds, wildflowers, and places of geological significance. The museum is open without charge Monday through Saturday from 9:00 a.m. to 4:30 p.m. and Sunday from 1:00 p.m. to 5:00 p.m.

The St. Johnsbury Athenaeum at 30 Main Street was built and given to the city by Horace Fairbanks, Thaddeus's nephew. Designed by John Davis Hatch of New York City, the building is another superlative example of Victorian architecture. The Athenaeum contains an excellent library and an art gallery lit by skylights in a domed ceiling. The gallery houses a permanent collection of nearly one hundred canvases, half being copies of European masterworks and half originals of the Hudson River School. Included are works by Jasper Cropsey, Asher B. Durand, James and William Hart, and Worthington Whittredge. But the *piece de resistance* remains the ten-by-fifteen-foot "Domes of the Yosemite" by Albert Bierstadt. When it was acquired, *The New York Times* lamented that "it is now doomed to the obscurity of a Vermont town where it will astonish the natives." To that, Fairbanks replied, "The people who live in this obscurity are nevertheless quite capable of appreciating the dignity it lends to this small village." Bierstadt was apparently not upset by the painting's location, for he returned every summer until his death to view it and retouch it. The Athenaeum is open without charge Monday and Friday from 10:00 a.m. to 8:00 p.m., Tuesday through Thursday from 10:00 a.m. to 5:00 p.m., and Saturday from 10:00 a.m. to 2:00 p.m. It is closed on Sundays and legal holidays.

As you leave St. Johnsbury on US 2, you pass the Maple Grove Maple Museum on your right. Here you can tour the world's largest maple sugar candy factory, see a movie showing how maple syrup is made—it takes forty gallons of sap to make one gallon of syrup—and visit an exhibit of sugarmaking equipment. If you decide to purchase some candy, examine the label closely to see whether you are getting pure maple sugar or a blend of maple and cane sugars. The museum is open from Memorial Day until late October seven days a week from 9:00 a.m. to 5:00 p.m. Admission is charged.

Most of the next five miles are a compromise. The eastern outskirts of St. Johnsbury along US 2 are congested and not pretty, but they form a necessary link in the route. If you have not yet eaten, buy some food at one of the markets on US 2 and carry it along for a picnic.

33.0 At Aimee's Restaurant—a pleasant place to eat if the weather is poor—turn RIGHT onto Route 18 South toward Lower Waterford. The road goes uphill for a mile and then levels off beside Stiles Pond. Traffic on Route 18 can get heavy, but not as heavy as on US 2.

36.0 At the sign for Waterford Sand & Gravel and the Waterford School, turn RIGHT off Route 18 onto the unsigned road.

39.0 At the gravel pit, continue STRAIGHT onto the unpaved road.

You follow unpaved roads for two and six-tenths miles from this turn.

40.4 At the T, turn LEFT and continue on the unpaved road.

41.6 At the Stop Sign, just after the road surface becomes paved again, go STRAIGHT.

Just before reaching the next turn, you ride through the hillside village of Lower Waterford. Several of its houses date to the eighteenth century, and the post office especially evokes scenes from another age. The Rabbit Hill Inn is located in Lower Waterford, but its excellent dining room does not serve lunch.

44.0 At the Stop Sign, turn RIGHT onto Route 18 South.

45.5 Just after crossing the Connecticut River into New Hampshire, turn RIGHT onto New Hampshire Route 135 South.

As you ride south on a ridge above the river, you can see Lower Waterford and Barnet rising out of the trees on the Vermont shore.

57.0 At the Exxon sign in Monroe, New Hampshire, turn RIGHT onto the unsigned road and ride across the Connecticut River back into Vermont. When you reach the stop sign at US 5, you will be in McIndoe Falls, where the tour began.

Bicycle Shops

Demers Repair, Inc., 81 South Main Street, Barre, VT   (802-476-7712)

Lyndon Cycle Shop, 72 Broad Street, Lyndon, VT   (802-626-5334)

Onion River Sports, 20 Langdon Street, Montpelier, VT   (802-229-9409)

Park Pedals, Town Highway II, Cabot, VT   (802-563-2252)

Progressive Sport, 84 Concord Avenue, St. Johnsbury, VT   (802-748-2986)

20

Lakes of the Northeast Kingdom: A three-day tour

The distance and terrain are stated at the beginning of each day's directions.

Vermont's northern Piedmont and glaciated Connecticut River highlands have been known as the Northeast Kingdom since former U.S. Senator George Aiken so dubbed them several years ago. This, the most sparsely settled region of the state, retains an ethereal quality, difficult to define, yet evident to those who take the time to explore it. This tour, beginning in East Burke, is designed to give you that opportunity.

Totaling as much as 155 miles over three days, the tour seeks out the deep glacial lakes, conifer forests, hill towns, and expansive overgrown farmlands that evoke the magnificent serenity for which the Kingdom is famous. Each day brings you to a sparkling lake—Island Pond, Lake Willoughby, Crystal Lake, and Lake Seymour—where swimming is a joy. On clear days from the hill towns of Sutton, Sheffield, and Holland you can view the White Mountains of New Hampshire as well as the Green Mountains of Vermont. Indeed, before leaving East Burke drive the toll road up Burke Mountain (el. 3,267'); frost heaves have buckled the road so badly it is not safe to descend by bicycle. At the top nothing obstructs your view, and with the aid of a map you can identify the major geological formations that you will soon be seeing by bicycle. The towns along the route offer less of architectural or historical interest than do those in the more prosperous sections of the state.

But you can plan your tour to coincide with a country fair in Barton or Lyndonville and can visit the home of the unique Bread and Puppet Theater. And wherever you are, the roads will be virtually free of traffic.

The tour is deliberately constructed to provide several choices. Actually, it is four tours: the first, a circular day trip between East Burke and Barton, described as Day One; the second a circular two-day tour between East Burke and Derby Line, consisting of Days Two and Three; the third, a three-day figure eight combining Days One, Two, and Three in that order; and the fourth, a Century, covering Days Two and Three in twelve hours. The tour is also designed so that you may use either country inns or campgrounds for lodging and so you encounter the most difficult rides when you can be free of your panniers.

Do not start this tour until you have contacted the places where you will sleep, for you cannot rely on their being prepared for you without notice. Unless you live nearby, you will surely find it convenient to stay in East Burke the night before you start bicycling. And, if you are camping, you can save time and eat better by bringing your food from home.

On the night before you begin cycling and the night between Days One and Two, stay at either the Old Cutter Inn (802-626-5152) or Darling State Park (no telephone). The mailing address for both is simply East Burke, VT 05832. If you cannot be accommodated, call Burke Mountain Recreation, Inc., for assistance 802-626-3305. The Old Cutter Inn provides attractive rooms with shared baths in its main building and with private baths in the Carriage House. My favorite rooms are #1, which has two double beds, cheerful, flowered wallpaper, lots of afternoon sunshine, and a bath down the hall, and #7, which faces Mounts Hor and Pisgah, and has two twin beds, its own bathroom, and an outdoor deck. Rooms rent for $18 to $24 per night, double occupancy, and innkeepers Fritz and Marti Walther serve breakfast as well as fine continental dinners. Vermont room and meals tax plus gratuity add 10 to 20 percent to these prices. The inn has a full liquor license, small bar, wood-beamed dining room, and splendid mountain view. The Old Cutter is closed on Mondays, and reservations are essential.

Darling State Park in East Burke opens the Friday preceding Memorial Day and closes October 12. The park provides a total of twenty-seven tent sites ($4.50 per day) and ten-by-thirteen-foot, three-sided, wooden floor lean-tos ($5.50 per day), hot showers, toilets, water, firewood, ice, and a small store. Vermont residents are charged $1.00 less per night. Vermont state parks do not accept reservations for less than six nights; space is distributed on a first-come, first-served basis.

On the night between Days Two and Three, you can stay at either Char-Bo Campground near Derby or Seymour Lake Lodge in Morgan Center. Char-Bo, a private campground and member of VAPCOO, opens May 15 and closes October 1. Owners Robert and Charlotte Knowles welcome reservations for a single night and may be reached at Char-Bo Campground, Box 54, Derby, VT 05829 (802-766-8807). Char-Bo offers swimming in Lake Salem, forty-two campsites at $4 and more per day, toilets, hot showers, and laundry facilities.

Seymour Lake Lodge is one of Vermont's most extraordinary inns. Simple to the point of rusticity, the Lodge nevertheless provides an unmatched welcome in the twinkling smile of grandmother-innkeeper Frances Oliver and in her unsurpassed Vermont cooking. No one knows better how to cheer a tired cyclist than Frances who has been serving fishermen and hunters for thirty years. It is difficult not to relax completely sitting before the fireplace in the living room or lounging on the lawn in the late afternoon sunshine as you gaze across Seymour Lake. The Lodge has no liquor license, and its eight rooms share two and a half baths. But Frances has not advertised in years—in fact I found her inn through the Morgan Town Clerk—so you could be the only guests. My favorite rooms are #7 and #8. Lodging, breakfast, and dinner are a bargain at about $20 per person including tax and gratuity. Frances Oliver is, however, approaching the conclusion of her career as an innkeeper. She may sell the lodge, and it might then change. You must make reservations by contacting Seymour Lake Lodge, Morgan Center, VT 05854 (802-895-2752). If you cannot be accommodated, see what Frances can suggest or get in touch with the Chamber of Commerce, Newport, VT 05855 (802-334-7782).

Day One

East Burke-Barton-East Burke: Moderate-to-difficult terrain; 50 miles

0.0 From either the Old Cutter Inn or Darling State Park, follow the Burke Mountain Recreation Area road downhill to East Burke.

2.5 At the Stop Sign in East Burke, turn LEFT onto Route 114 South.

In a hundred yards you pass a grocery on the right and a general store on the left. The classic general store contains the East Burke post office and sells food, hardware, and dry goods. Get your snacks either here in East Burke or in five miles at Lyndonville, for afterwards little is available until you reach Barton.

East Burke's Old School Museum stands two hundred yards south of the general store on the same side of the road. This eighteen-by-twenty-three foot retired schoolhouse contains a potpourri of items from its past: primers, pupils' desks, musical instruments, and a globe made around 1800 by a local resident. The building is neither electrified nor heated and opens only during daylight hours on mild days from June to October. If the door is locked, you can get a key from the caretaker who lives in the white house next door.

7.5 At the blinker on the outskirts of Lyndonville, go STRAIGHT onto US 5 South.

7.8 At the next blinker, which is in Lyndonville, go STRAIGHT off US 5 onto the unsigned road.

If you have not yet gotten food, stop at White Market, on your left at this light.

The Cobleigh Public Library in Lyndonville contains an interesting collection of Vermontiana, old coins, stuffed New England birds, and an eighteenth-century grandfather's clock. The library is open Monday through Saturday from 1:30 p.m. to 5:30 p.m. On Wednesday evenings during the summer, the Lyndonville band performs at the bandstand in Powers Park across from White Market. And the Caledonia County Fair, which in true Vermont style combines livestock and agricultural exhibitions with the attractions of a traveling carnival, happens at Lyndonville during August. For further information about the fair, contact the Lyndonville Town Clerk, 24 Main Street, Lyndonville, VT 05851 (802-626-5785).

8.0 At the Stop Sign in Lyndonville, turn RIGHT and follow the signs for Route 122 North.

You pass Lyndon Institute, a coeducational boarding secondary school, on your left, go through Miller's Run covered bridge (1878), and then bear left onto Route 122—all within three-quarters of a mile.

A mile beyond Wheelock, Route 122 begins working its way uphill through Sheffield for three and a half miles. The grade begins gently but turns steep in the last mile. The top of the hill marks the Connecticut River-Lake Champlain watershed; most rivers to the east flow into the former, while those to the west flow into the latter. Pause to look behind you at the view, for on some days you can see all the way to New Hampshire's Mount Washington. Then enjoy the two-and-a-half-mile downhill run that lies ahead.

In 1785, during Vermont's brief tenure as an independent nation (1777-91), the General Assembly took the unusual action of granting land to a college in another country. Having no college of its own and wishing to insure its sons' opportunities for learning, Vermont granted half the township of Wheelock to New Hampshire's Dartmouth College. As late as 1815 the rentals Wheelock townspeople paid to Dartmouth accounted for a major portion of the college's revenues. Wheelock still pays a small annual sum to Dartmouth. In return the college charges no tuition to those sons and, more recently, daughters of Wheelock who qualify for admission.

About a mile down the hill toward Route 16 you pass on your right the home of the Bread and Puppet Theater. This innovative company, which has toured widely in the United States and abroad, uses gigantic masks, hand puppets, and mime in forceful, often political dramatizations, which are frequently performed on the street. Guests are welcome to stop and see the company's puppets.

23.0   At the Stop Sign, turn RIGHT onto Route 16 North.

In three miles you pass the Barton Fairgrounds on your left. It's worth slowing down to see what is going on. Some of the major shows exhibited here are: the Memorial Day Horse Show, a Fourth of July celebration, the Arts and Crafts Show in early August, and the Orleans County Fair in mid-August. For information about these or other attractions contact the Chamber of Commerce, Barton, VT 05822 (802-525-6210).

27.0   At the intersection in Barton, turn RIGHT onto US 5 South.

Since no stores fall along the next fifteen miles of your path, make certain you have what you want before leaving. If you carry your lunch along, you can picnic within a few miles on the shore of Crystal Lake. The best places to reach the water for swimming are at the fishing accesses.

34.0   One-quarter mile past a small lumber mill and Bean Pond on your left, turn RIGHT off US 5 onto the road to Sutton. (Look carefully for this turn; it is easy to miss.)

As soon as you turn you pass beneath a railroad trestle and begin to climb a formidable hill. About a mile up you can refill your water bottle at a mountain spring on the right. The grade of the hill tapers off a short way past the spring and remains gradual for another two miles. On the top you cycle along a plateau, from which the views eastward are superb, for roughly a mile before gliding downhill into Sutton.

39.0   Immediately after passing the Sutton Elementary School—partially obscured by foliage on your right—turn LEFT toward West Burke at the intersection beside a tan, imitation-brick house on the left. (Try to approach this turn slowly, for it too is easy to miss.)

The road from Sutton goes downhill for a half-mile, up for three-quarters, and down the rest of the way to West Burke. It offers exceptional views of Burke Mountain off to your right, but keep your eye on the road during the final descent, for it is fast, and suddenly curves ninety degrees to the left.

41.8 After crossing the railroad tracks on the outskirts of West Burke, bear LEFT onto the unsigned road.

42.0 At the Stop Sign in West Burke, turn RIGHT onto US 5 South, go just past the K & G Market (on the left), and then turn LEFT onto Route 5A North. In seventy-five yards, as soon as you cross a bridge, turn RIGHT off Route 5A onto the road toward Burke Hollow and East Burke. Then immediately bear RIGHT at the fork. (All these turns occur within a quarter-mile.)

The ride from West Burke through Burke Hollow can be arduous after all the cycling you have done. You must climb a gradual three-quarter-mile-long hill in the first two miles and then a very steep one of the same length just beyond Burke Hollow. The second climb ends by a cemetery and gives way to an easy, occasionally downhill, ride into East Burke.

The Union Meeting House, which sends its delicate spire high above the rooftops of Burke Hollow, remains unaltered, save fresh white paint, since its construction in 1825. It is worth stopping—either now or tomorrow when you come by again— to see the old box pews, each with its own door, and the high barrel pulpit.

47.1 At the Yield Sign on the edge of East Burke, turn LEFT onto the unsigned road and ride a tenth of a mile across the bridge.

47.2 At the Stop Sign in East Burke, turn LEFT onto Route 114 North.

47.5 At the sign for Burke Mountain Recreation Area, turn RIGHT onto the road to the Old Cutter Inn and Darling State Park.

As you may recall, this hill is unrelenting, but the grade is moderate to gentle most of the way.

50.0 You are back at your starting point.

Day Two

East Burke to Seymour Lake Lodge: moderate terrain; 51 miles

East Burke to Char-Bo Campground direct: easy-to-moderate terrain; 31 miles

East Burke to Char-Bo Campground via Morgan Center: moderate terrain; 60 miles

0.0 From either the Old Cutter Inn or Darling State Park, follow the Burke Mountain Recreation Area road downhill to East Burke.

Before you start bicycling, find a vantage point with an unobstructed view to the north. There, slightly to the west of north, you can see the prominent, hummocklike peaks of Mounts Hor and Pisgah. They define the glacial canyon within which lies Lake Willoughby and through which you will soon be riding.

2.5   At the Stop Sign in East Burke, turn LEFT onto Route 114 South.

Buy some food for snacks and a picnic lunch at one of the two stores in East Burke. Though you can get something to drink at the store in Westmore, the choice of foods there leaves much to be desired. If you are planning to take the thirty-one-mile route to Char-Bo Campground, consider buying your dinner and breakfast groceries in East Burke. The stores along your route offer only the bare essentials.

2.8   By the Old School Museum (on the left), turn RIGHT toward Burke Hollow and West Burke. Go across the bridge and then turn RIGHT toward Burke Hollow.

You are leaving East Burke by the roads you returned on yesterday. For the first mile and a half you climb a gentle grade. Then, from the cemetery on your right, you descend quickly three-quarters of a mile into Burke Hollow.

5.5   Just past the Union Meeting House (on the right) in Burke Hollow, bear LEFT and then immediately bear RIGHT to follow the main road to West Burke.

Yesterday's climb is now a descent which makes the two miles to West Burke an easy ride.

7.5   At the Stop Sign in West Burke, turn RIGHT onto Route 5A North.

If you still need food or supplies, turn left at this Stop Sign and ride a tenth of a mile to the two stores in West Burke. Route 5A stays flat until it passes the northern end of Lake Willoughby, when it goes up a moderately steep hill for a mile and a half.

Set directly between the rocky faces of Mounts Hor (el. 2,751′) and Pisgah (el. 2,646′), Lake Willoughby measures six miles from north to south and 600′ deep. Its strikingly clear waters make excellent swimming as well as fishing and can be reached most easily from beaches at its northern and southern ends. The largest fish known to be caught in Vermont waters came from Lake Willoughby. A forty-six-inch lake trout with a girth of twenty-five inches, it weighed thirty-four pounds. Leon E. Hopkins, who beached the trophy on May 6, 1960, had it mounted, and it hangs on the wall of his insurance agency in Lyndonville.

By a quirk of nature, rare, delicate Arctic plants grow on the cliffs of Mount Pisgah. Mostly calcicoles, which take the calcium they need from the rocks they cling to, these relics of the Ice Age find the moist, protected ledges of Pisgah hospitable. A hiking trail leads to the summit of Mount Pisgah from the east side of Route 5A, a half-mile south of the southern tip of Lake Willoughby. About seven miles round-trip, the hike is moderately difficult and takes approximately four and a half hours.

27.0   At the Stop Sign outside West Charleston, turn LEFT onto Routes 5A North and 105 West.

Before setting out toward West Charleston, take a moment to look at the Great Falls of the Clyde River. Directly across Route 105 from this Stop Sign, the Clyde River crashes through a gorge in a series of tumbling falls and high cascades. In the spring you may even see large rainbow trout negotiating the falls during their spawning runs.

Irving Dane's General Store in West Charleston—on your left in a mile—is the last place to shop on the thirty-one-mile route to Char-Bo Campground. The area between West Charleston and Derby was a favorite hunting ground of the St. Francis Indians. Routes 5A and 105 follow a gently rolling course.

31.0   The entrance to Char-Bo Campground a quarter-mile off the road is on your right.

If you are taking the sixty-mile route, you might want to stop at the campground to unburden yourself of your heavier gear. But remember to take along some packing equipment if you intend to pick up supplies before your return. The next twenty-nine miles pose a greater challenge than the first thirty-one.

33.5   At the intersection in Derby Center, go STRAIGHT onto US 5 North.

34.7   By Ev's Drive-in Restaurant (on the right), turn LEFT off US 5 onto the road toward Beebe Plain.

Cycling along Lake Willoughby with Mount Hor in the background

If you are hungry, try Ev's homemade brownies or turn-overs.

37.2 At the first intersection with a paved road, turn RIGHT onto the unsigned road.

Immediately after turning, you must climb a steep hill three-quarters of a mile long.

39.0 At the Stop Sign beside St. Edward's Church on the outskirts of Derby Line, turn LEFT onto US 5 North.

39.5 At the blinker in Derby Line, turn RIGHT toward Interstate 91.

If you would like to cross the border into Canada, this is the most convenient place to do so. Take along some identification in case U.S. Customs requests something when you return and simply go straight from this blinker a hundred yards into Quebec. The Opera House and Haskell Free Library in Derby Line exemplify the casual view often taken of the international border in this part of the country. The books in the library and the stage of the Opera House lie in one country while the check-out desk and the audience remain in the other.

If Seymour Lake Lodge is your destination for the day and you would like a drink when you arrive, buy your beer or wine in Derby Line, for it is the last chance you have. Also be sure you have all the food you want for the final eleven and a half miles, for not a single store sits along your route between Derby Line and Morgan Center, and the ride is not easy. From Derby Line to the crossroad that marks Holland, you climb 400' in elevation along roads that roll more up than down over moderately steep, short hills.

46.0 At the intersection one-half mile past the Holland Elementary School (on the left), turn RIGHT onto the unsigned road.

The balance of the ride to Morgan Center goes mostly downhill and near the end provides a lovely long view of Seymour Lake. One of the two or three largest lakes fully within Vermont, Seymour contains water so pure the State Department of Health has approved it for drinking.

51.0 At the Stop Sign in Morgan Center, you are facing Seymour Lake. Immediately to your left is the Seymour Lake Lodge where you end the day's ride unless you are camping. If you are following the sixty-mile route to Char-Bo Campground, turn RIGHT at this Stop Sign onto Route 111 West.

Route 111 looks in contour like the teeth of a rip-saw. For four miles the road rolls relentlessly up and down short, steep hills.

55.0   At the second intersection with a paved road on the left, which comes two miles beyond The Morgan Store (on the left), turn LEFT onto the unsigned road. (A sign for West Charleston is posted at this turn, but it faces away from you and consequently is not visible until after you have made the left turn.)

The Morgan Store stocks an excellent supply of fresh meats and groceries, some produce, beer, and wine—plenty to fill your panniers for dinner and breakfast at the campground. In a half-mile, the road to West Charleston becomes unpaved for a half-mile, but the surface is smooth and firm and, like the rest of this road, slopes gently downward.

57.0   At the Stop Sign in West Charleston, turn RIGHT onto Route 5A North and 105 West.

60.0   The entrance to Char-Bo Campground leads off Route 105 to your right.

Day Three

Seymour Lake Lodge to East Burke: moderate terrain; 54 or 44 miles

Char-Bo Campground to East Burke: easy-to-moderate terrain; 42 or 32 miles

0.0   From Seymour Lake Lodge, turn RIGHT onto Route 111 West.

Over the first four miles Route 111 rolls over short, steep hills shaped like the teeth of a rip-saw. The last five miles, leading into Derby Center, also roll, but less frequently and more gently. You can buy something to carry along for a snack at The Morgan Store, two miles from Seymour Lake Lodge on the left side of Route 111.

9.0   At the Stop Sign in Derby Center, turn LEFT onto Routes 5A South and 105 East.

The next seven miles follow roads you cycled yesterday in the opposite direction.

12.0   From Char-Bo Campground, turn LEFT onto Routes 5A South
(0.0)   and 105 East.

For the next four miles you cycle along roads that yesterday
you rode in the opposite direction.

16.0   At the fork one mile south of West Charleston, bear LEFT onto
(4.0)   Route 105 East toward Island Pond.

In a mile and a half you ride up a gradual mile-long hill and then
descend for the same distance. Another mile and a half brings
you to East Charleston, where you can select snacks or food for
a picnic from a good selection at the East Charleston Store, on
the right.

26.0   At the intersection of Routes 105 and 114, go STRAIGHT onto
(14.0) Routes 105 East and 114 North toward Island Pond.

If you would like to shorten your tour by ten miles—and skip
the ride which circles Island Pond—do not go straight at this
intersection. Instead, turn right onto Route 114 South and continue according to the directions below from mileage 36.0 (24.0).
If you take the short cut be sure that you have all the food and
drink you want; nothing is available on Route 114.

28.0   At the Stop Sign in Island Pond, which is the name of both the
(16.0) town and the lake, turn RIGHT onto Route 105 East.

Before leaving town, be certain you have all the food you want
for the balance of the day, for there is nowhere to shop again
until you reach East Burke.

30.0   One-half mile past Ken and Barb's Lakeside Camping (on the
(18.0) right), turn RIGHT off Route 105 onto the road toward Brighton
State Park.

31.0   The lawn at Brighton State Park stretches one hundred fifty
(19.0) yards from the right side of the road to the beach on Island Pond.

The park supplies changing rooms, toilets, picnic tables, and a
lifeguard; admission is $.75. Island Pond takes its name from the
twenty-two acre island in its center. The swimming is excellent,
and the park makes a delightful picnic spot. After stopping,
continue bicycling in the direction you were headed.

32.0   At the T, turn RIGHT onto the unsigned road.
(20.0)

34.0   At the T, turn LEFT onto Routes 114 South and 105 West.
(22.0)

36.0   At the intersection, turn LEFT to continue on Route 114 South
(24.0)   toward Burke Mountain.

         If you are looking for a picnic spot, try the lawn by the Methodist
Church on the right in East Haven, nine miles south of this
intersection. The first two and a half miles of Route 114 climb
steadily to the top of a hill which then gives way to a delightful
three-mile descent. From there through East Haven to East
Burke, the terrain remains flat, and the cycling is easy unless
a headwind strikes you.

51.5   At the sign for Burke Mountain Recreation Area (on the left) just
(39.5)   outside the village of East Burke, turn LEFT onto the road to the
Old Cutter Inn and Darling State Park.

54.0   You are back where you began your tour, and now as you look out
(42.0)   toward Willoughby Gap perhaps you understand a little of the
mystery of Vermont's Northeast Kingdom.

Bicycle Shops

Lyndon Cycle Shop, 72 Broad Street, Lyndon, VT   (802-626-5334)

Motion Sports, Route 105, Newport Center, VT   (802-334-7029)

Onion River Sports, 20 Langdon Street, Montpelier, VT   (802-229-9409)

Park Pedals, Town Highway II, Cabot, VT   (802-563-2252)

Progressive Sport, 84 Concord Avenue, St. Johnsbury, VT   (802-748-2986)

Appendix

Anybody's Bike Book, by Tom Cuthbertson, (Ten Speed Press, Berkeley, CA; 1971) is a cleverly written, reliable, and informal guide to bicycle repair.

Bicycling
33 East Minor Street
Emmaus, PA 18049

Bicycling is a monthly magazine featuring articles about bicycle equipment, conditioning, touring, racing, and technical and medical topics. Its ads are an excellent source of information about bicycle retailers, book clubs, and tours.

Bikecentennial
P.O. Box 8308
Missoula, MT 59807

Bikecentennial is a member-supported bicyclists' resource center. Since inaugurating the TransAmerica Trail in 1976, Bikecentennial has continued to develop a nationwide network of long cycling trails, to publish excellent guidebooks to the trails, and to distribute its own fine pamphlets on topics of concern to touring cyclists.

Bike World
P.O. Box 366
Mountain View, CA 94042

Bike World is a bi-monthly magazine dealing with the same sorts of topics as *Bicycling*.

Bike Tripping, by Tom Cuthbertson, (Ten Speed Press, Berkeley, CA; 1972) is another witty statement by Cuthbertson this time offering advice on "how to have a good trip on a bike." It also includes valuable information, especially in the chapter on frame building by master craftsman, Albert Eisentraut.

Glenn's Complete Bicycle Manual, by Clarence W. Coles and Harold T. Glenn, (Crown Publishers, Inc., New York; 1973) guides you comprehensively through the mysterious worlds of bicycle selection, maintenance, and repair. This book is filled with clear, helpful illustrations.

DeLong's Guide to Bicycles & Bicycling, by Fred DeLong, (Chilton Book Company, Radnor, PA; 1974) is the encyclopedic statement about bicycle hardware and the art of cycling by one of bicycling's technical wizards. The book is well illustrated and indexed.

League of American Wheelmen
19 South Bothwell
Palatine, IL 60067

The LAW is a national organization of affiliated bicycle clubs, which jointly and independently run many day trips and bicycle rallies. Members, whose dues support the League, receive a monthly magazine filled with news of club-sponsored events. LAW also tries to represent cyclists' interests to legislators and public agencies.

Vermont Agency of Development and Community Affairs
61 Elm Street
Montpelier, VT 05672 (802-828-3236)

This is the source for the official state highway map and other information of use to visitors.

Vermont Bicycle Touring
R.D. 2B
Bristol, VT 05443 (802-388-4011)

Founded by the author in 1972, VBT runs inn-to-inn bicycle tours for adults and families. The tours range in length from a weekend to twenty-eight days, are rated according to difficulty, and are guided by leaders who are good mechanics. VBT also runs a five-day bicycle repair clinic and rents ten-speed bicycles.

Guidebooks from New Hampshire Publishing Company

Written for people of all ages and experience, these highly popular and carefully prepared books feature detailed directions, notes on points of interest, sketch maps, and photographs.

For bicyclists—

20 Bicycle Tours in New Hampshire, by Tom and Susan Heavey. $5.95
20 Bicycle Tours in Vermont, by John S. Freidin. $5.95

About Vermont—

25 Ski Tours in the Green Mountains, by Sally and Daniel Ford. $4.95
Fifty Hikes in Vermont, by Ruth and Paul Sadlier. $6.95
Canoe Camping Vermont and New Hampshire Rivers, by Roioli Schweiker. $4.95
A Year with New England's Birds: Twenty-five Field Trips, by Sandy Mallett. $5.95

Other guides—

Fifty Hikes in Central Pennsylvania, by Tom Thwaites. $6.95
25 Ski Tours in the Northern Adirondacks, by Richard Beamish (Fall 1979). $4.95
Fifty Hikes in the White Mountains, by Daniel Doan. $6.95

Available from bookstores, sporting goods stores, or the publisher. For a complete description of these and other guides in the *Fifty Hikes, 25 Walks,* and *25 Ski Tours* series, write: New Hampshire Publishing Co., Box 70, Somersworth, NH 03878.